FIRST THE BLACK HORSE

by

Robert Underhill

DORRANCE PUBLISHING CO., INC.
PITTSBURGH, PENNSYLVANIA 15222

The opinions expressed herein are those of the author, who assumes complete and sole responsibility for them, and do not necessarily represent the views of the publisher or its agents.

Dorrance Publishing Co., Inc.
701 Smithfield Street
Pittsburgh, PA 15222
Visit our website at *www.dorrancebookstore.com*

ISBN: 978-1-4349-1050-9
eISBN: 978-1-4349-5910-2

To my beloved daughter, Sandy, who guided the preparation of this book but passed away before it was published.

The four horsemen of the Apocalypse in the Bible are allegorical figures. The rider on the white horse has many interpretations, one of which is Christ. The rider on the red horse is war; on the black horse, famine; and on the pale horse, death.
Columbia Encyclopedia, 2nd. Ed., p. 706.

ACKNOWLEDGMENTS

Acknowledgments provide an author opportunity to thank those who made his book possible, and offering them is a more pleasurable task than other writing.

My book grows from several decades of students and fellow faculty members who, through discussions, coffee klatsches, classes, and seminars have contributed directly or indirectly.

Librarians and research specialists also have given valuable assistance. Those at the William R. Parks Library on the Iowa State campus have been especially helpful. There I've had the privilege of a carrel for private work space and secure storage for selected books and related material. I've also been helped by library aides at the FDR Library in Hyde Park, N.Y., the Truman Library at Independence, Mo., and regular personnel at the Ames Public Library. All have been courteous and ready to accommodate my requests.

A book is a cooperative venture between author and publisher, and I would be remiss if I failed to acknowledge the excellent work of Dorrance Publishing. Assistants with that firm have given good guidance and answered my questions quickly.

To me, computers are mysteries yet to be solved, and although I use mine constantly it continues to baffle me. One wrong key and a new message appears; composing is halted until a remedy is found. If I can't find one, which is usually the case, I call on my friend and computer whiz, Professor Herb Harmison. Herb comes in and with one or two strokes has me back on track. Without Herb my computer would be worthless; with his knowledge and help it is invaluable.

Several friends have followed the manuscript, and they include Fred and Terry Schlunz, who are patient in listening to ideas and even trial passages before I write them. Another good friend and confidant is Margaret Maitland, who grew up in the time span dealt with in this book and has professed interest in its development.

On a more personal level, I owe more to my two daughters, Susan and Sandy, than I can ever express let alone repay. Sandy's courage despite adversities was an inspiration, and no one could have followed my daily progress more carefully than she. Unfortunately, Sandy passed away between completion of the manuscript and its publication, but without her devotion the work would not have been undertaken. I trust she understands the book is a tribute to her.

My daughter Sue has been monitor, critic, and editor-in-chief. She has fine editorial judgment honed by her teaching experiences. Sue read the manuscript in its entirety. When she read a chapter and found me rambling or passages out of place, she would brush aside nostalgic cobwebs and urge me to get back to historical facts—facts which I hope each reader finds interesting and pertinent.

Robert Underhill

TABLE OF CONTENTS

PRELUDE

Any oldster can tell you that ten years is but a dollop of time, for a decade races past quickly. Yet in that span, a boy's freckles will give way to whiskers and a spindly stick of a girl can change into a curvaceous woman. Society's changes are not always immediately noticeable, but they occur, nevertheless, and have wider and more lasting effects than what happens to individuals.

Some decades are more deeply etched in history than others. It took less than ten years—356 B.C. to 346 B.C.—for Alexander the Great to conquer most of the civilized world in his time. In the years between 58 B.C. and 49 B.C., Julius Caesar won enough victories in the Gallic Wars to establish his honors for rule of the Roman Empire.

In the ten years between 1780 and 1790 A.D., thirteen disparate colonies on the American continent separated from England, and a new nation was conceived. Seventy years later, when Abraham Lincoln spoke at Gettysburg, the country's population was 35 million. The dominating events in the ten years between 1860 and 1870 were both Lincoln's emergence as a leader and his death.

Seventy years would pass before our nation would face a disaster as threatening to our home as the one it had overcome in the Civil War period. Near the end of the 1920s, prosperity evaporated, and in the ten years between 1930 and 1940, the United States suffered a Great Depression. Stocks plummeted, financial institutions failed, homes were lost, and more than 13 million wage earners, 10 percent of the entire citizenry then, were unemployed. In the bleak year of 1932, banks, overrun by nervous depositors, many of whom already had lost part or all of their savings, closed their doors, and in cities, bread lines and soup kitchens were organized. Just outside city limits were shantytowns, or dump heaps, where vagrants huddled in common misery. In small towns and on farms, existence was equally difficult. Toil was relentless as men and women tried to eke out a meager living, just enough to feed and clothe their children.

Everyone worried, searched for answers, and found only more questions. Economic woes upset many traditional beliefs and values. Extremists on both right and left preached nostrums, which some listeners readily accepted. Prohibition had not driven out drink as prophesied; indeed, speakeasies—visited by upstanding citizens who might attend a favorite haunt and maintain that other places were nothing but dens of iniquity—flourished. Rat-infested tenements existed in every city, for squalor was everywhere. Poverty helped bring on new crimes, and a class of criminals—glorified by newspapers, radio, and Hollywood—extended fiefdoms beyond local neighborhoods.

Jobs were lost, and scapegoats had to be found. Those might be greedy employers, foreigners, negroes[1], scabs, or strangers of any sort; it didn't matter. Labor unions had grown since the turn of the century, and these organizations renewed their efforts on behalf of both skilled and unskilled workers.

Questions grew like weeds about beliefs which had been followed in the period immediately after the first World War—a period during which many U.S. citizens were told "we had no business getting into it in the first place."

The role of government set off debates and controversies. Most were conservatives, believers in traditional economists, such as Adam Smith. Operating under different organizational titles, they argued *laissez faire* theories, "the business of America is business" and "the best government is one which governs least." On the other side were proponents who saw government as the only agency that could save the nation. Adherents in this group rejected Smith's theses and adopted those of John Maynard Keynes, a British economist who didn't worry about government deficits but saw advantages in using public monies for the purpose of stimulating private business, called pump priming.

While America wrestled with economic and moral uncertainties, skies throughout the world darkened as war clouds formed—a few of them bursting to expose worsening troubles. In 1936 and 1937, Japan, with almost unbelievable barbarism, invaded China. Civil war broke out in Spain, and Italy invaded Ethiopia. Then in the fall of 1939, German Chancellor Adolph Hitler ordered Nazi troops to cross the Oder River into neighboring Poland, and World War II began.

In slightly more than a decade, a gigantic change occurred. America rose from being one of several noted democratic governments to be indisputably the leading financial, industrial, and military power in the world.

Modern historians and economists disagree over whether the Great Depression was ended primarily by New Deal measures or by increased rearmament programs in America and around the world.

This book will let the reader decide.

---

[*] In the period described in this book, the term "negroes" or "colored" were accepted usages; the term "blacks" would have been highly pejorative.

FIRST THE BLACK HORSE
BOOK I: STATE OF THE NATION
CHAPTER 1: PRIOR TO 1930

Erie County, Pennsylvania, in 1863, and Cleveland, Ohio, its neighbor slightly farther west on the shores of Lake Erie, were filled with dynamic young men struggling to get ahead. Oil deposits had been discovered in the region, and one thousand dollars or less might be enough to start drilling, put up a small refinery, and hire workers to run it. John D. Rockefeller, not yet the titan he would become, was capturing oil wells and buying railroad lines that transported their "crude" product.[1]

Many of those who moved westward were men and women recently arrived in America. No official records were made of the influx of immigrants coming to the new nation prior to 1820; however, authorities estimate the number between the close of the Revolutionary War and that year must have been close to 250,000.

The great potato blight struck Ireland in the 1840s when that country's population was about 8,500,000. More than a million Irish citizens died of starvation and disease within a five-year period, and in the seven years between 1847 and 1854, no less than 1,000,000 emigrated from Ireland to the United States. Looked down upon by established residents, the recent immigrants took any job available—most often the lowest paid ones with railroads, mines, or taverns. Often shunned and lumped together, society called them "shanty Irish" or "Micks."

Other immigrants came, too. There were Chinese, Japanese, and a few from Mexico or South American countries. In the nine years between 1911 and 1920—the period of the First World War—more than 5,736,000 responded to the poem Emma Lazarus had written to be inscribed on the Statue of Liberty—

Give me your tired, your poor,
Your huddled masses yearning to breathe free,
The wretched refuse of your teeming shore. . .

Reliable records show that 241,700 aliens were admitted to the U.S. in the single year of 1930, and the total number of immigrants for the next ten years would be slightly more than twice that figure.[2]

IMMIGRATION BY DECADES [3]

Period	Number
1820-1830	151,824
1831-1840	869, 920
1841-1850	1,713,251
1851-1860	2,598,214
1861-1870	2,314,824
1871-1880	2,812,191
1881-1890	5,246,613
1891-1900	3,687,564
1901-1910	8,795,386
1911-1920	5,735,811
1921-1930	4,107,109
1931-1939	829,980

In the decade beginning in 1920, the number of immigrants coming to America declined and immigration laws became more restrictive. Then, during the desperate years of 1931 to 1940, the number of newcomers fell dramatically to less than 528,000 per annum.

For two decades following the first World War, immigrations plunged, the total number of new arrivals to just over 4,000,000 for a ten-year period. Immigration laws became more restrictive. Persons whose religions differed, whose eyes might be more slanted, or whose skin color was black, brown, yellow, or tan had few jobs worthy of the name. They wore discarded clothing, lived in shanties, and suffered all sorts of insults and indignities. Moreover, during the 1920s throughout the North, South, and Midwest, the Ku Klux Klan incited violence against Catholics, Jews, and other minorities.

Many immigrants worked on railroad section gangs as iron rails wound their way into ever more depots. The first two decades of the twentieth century was a bonanza period for American railroading, and by 1930 the vast network of tracks linked the country from sea to sea. The lines not only carried more freight but transported twice as many persons as in 1900. Besides carrying more passengers, the rails moved them over greater distances. Figures for "passenger miles" tripled in ten years. Huge railroad corporations were formed—New York Central, Pennsylvania, Union Pacific, and Northern Pacific, to name a few.

In the bigger cities, electric trolley lines replaced horse-drawn vehicles. Interurban trolleys ran popular routes from major cities to smaller towns surrounding them. There was "Berkshire Hills," a luxurious, cream-colored trolley with buff trim and gold-leaf lettering, wicker seats, and red-brocaded curtains that ran between Great Barrington, Massachusetts, and Bennington, Vermont.

Commuters from the south side of Chicago could go into the Loop on the hour via Illinois Central trains. From areas north and east of the Windy City, there were electric trolleys—clean, fast, and comfortable. For example, steel workers in the plants of Gary, Indiana, could board the South Shore Line and be on Randolph Street in downtown Chicago within an hour.

It was the morning of the electrical age. Fifty years earlier, on March 31, 1880, Wabash, Indiana had made news by becoming the first electrically-lighted city in the world, but by 1930 most other cities of size had adopted the practice. Countless dynamos and turbines had been built, and transmission lines carried the magic power far and wide. In 1889, less than 2 percent of the power used in American industry came from electricity; by 1930, nearly half of it came from that source.

WWI had ended with the signing of the armistice on November 11, 1918, and two years later, Warren G. Harding was elected to the presidency. Upon Harding's death, Vice President Calvin Coolidge inherited the office. Coolidge, according to acerbic-tongued Alice Longworth Roosevelt, looked as if "he had been weaned on a pickle."

There had been a Red Scare during the Coolidge administration in which 2,700 suspected Communists, anarchists, and other radicals were arrested in a five-month period between January and May. Many were arrested during those frenzied months merely because they had strange names or spoke little English, and, as is so often the case, it was shadows rather than the object itself which caused the scare. Fears were more dangerous to American citizens than the Red Revolution in Russia.

On the whole, however, the 1920s were rosy in America as the nation recovered from a war which had promised to save the world for democracy. The decade featured Rudy Vallee crooning over the marvel of radio, flappers, speakeasies, bootleggers, bobbed hair, and illegal gin[2].

In 1920, women gained the right to vote, and on the warm sands of American beaches, girls pulled down shoulder straps of their bathing suits in order to acquire tanned backs, while wondering if it were true as fashion journals asserted that an evening gown must reach all the way to the ground.

Fortunes were made by gamblers on Wall Street. Up and up the market soared, gaining speed and spinning off miracles as it went. In the first week of September 1929, the nation's markets reached their glittering peak. Every Wall Street wiseacre, supposedly persons most knowledgeable about intricacies of investments, predicted the Bull Market would go on and on.

The downfall began on October 24, 1929, a day that came to be known as "Black Thursday." It was a misnomer, for that date was only the beginning; worse times lay ahead. There was a series of small gains as major financiers attempted to shore up markets, but their efforts brought only temporary relief. The expected recovery failed to appear, and stocks kept going down, down, and down. Oct. 29th, 1929, five days after Black Thursday, marked the end of past prosperity, and prices plummeted. Stock losses for 1929-31 were estimated at 50 billion; the Coolidge-Hoover heyday was not yet dead, but it was dying. With the big Bull Market gone, there was hardly an American whose life would not be changed. The time called for new ideas, new thoughts, courage, and stamina, as well as different moral values. In New York City, where the gigantic Empire State Building was being started, reverberations from the stock market crash were especially threatening. When the decade of the 1930s opened, there had been keen rivalry for title of the world's tallest building, and two other projects under construction in the city were competing for such recognition. The site chosen for the historic new building had been a farmstead in the late eighteenth century, but a hundred years later the urban block was occupied by the sumptuous Waldorf Astoria Hotel, frequented by the upper Four Hundred and social elite of the city.

Digging commenced the first month of 1930, with the actual building officially begun on St. Patrick's Day, when, among the dignitaries, former Governor Alfred E. Smith, designated as president of the construction corporation, wielded ceremonial shovels. Notwithstanding the widening Depression, work on the 102-story building progressed rapidly, and the structure was completed 410 days after its start.

On the first day of May, 1931, U.S. President Herbert Hoover pushed a button in Washington, D.C. to turn on lights of the Empire State Building—the world's tallest structure then. The building became an icon of American culture, featured in newspaper stories, news reels, and Hollywood movies. One famous film, *King Kong,* released in 1933, showed a gigantic ape, the title character, climbing the outside of the building to escape captors and fight off attacking airplanes before falling to his death.

Two years after the 1929 crash, faith in the Republican Party fell as badly as *Kong* and as fast as numbers posted by call boys on the market boards of Wall Street. President Hoover would be in office for another two years, but congressional elections came up in November, and on the fourth of that month, Republicans suffered their first setback since 1916. The GOP was able to maintain a razor thin majority in the Senate where the party claimed 48 adherents to 47 Democrats; one Senator was an Independent. In the House, it was equally close, with Republicans listing 218 members to 216 for the Democrats, and one Representative identifying himself as an Independent. Because of deaths and the single Independent, Democrats gained the eventual victory, enabling them to organize the House at the opening of the seventy-second Congress in the spring of 1931.

Congressional shifts were not the only changes occurring in America as the decade of the 1930s began.

Chapter 2: Hard Times

When Franklin Delano Roosevelt took office in March 1933, the nation's population had risen to approximately 130 million, and the thirteen colonies had become a government of forty-eight states. The decade beginning in 1930 was an epochal one, for during it the United States suffered its worst depression, endured industrial malaise, and came through a prelude to the most momentous war in the world's history. It was a decade to be remembered by more than just old men and women or glassy-eyed historical scholars.

The face of America changed as the Depression generated a new westward movement, especially by families from the stricken dust bowls of the Great Plains. Some of the larger cities in the East—Philadelphia, Cleveland, Boston, Newark, and St. Louis—showed decreases in population as residents fled to villages or farms. Notwithstanding the exodus from northern urban centers, southern industrial cities, like Birmingham, grew faster than before.

The west coast, however, was the strongest magnet. The population of Los Angeles led the growth, showing an increase from 1,238,048 to 1,504,277 in less than ten years. Other cities in southern California also swelled, but not with the spectacular figures of Los Angeles. Farther north, populations in California coastal cities, such as San Francisco, Oakland, and Sacramento, remained almost stationary.[1]

In 1932, when thirteen million American men and women could find no work, banks collapsed by the score, robbing depositors of dollars they had earned and had thought they were saving. Bustling factories, which a few years earlier had striven to fill orders, laid off their workers, locked gates, and closed—many forever. In cities, soup kitchens and bread lines kept some of the unemployed alive, but just barely. On the margins of once prosperous urban districts, wretched shantytowns grew like weeds. Across the country, parents and children were going to bed hungry, and no one understood how it could happen in such a rich, formerly-thriving nation. President Hoover was maligned as villain of it all, and debasing limericks about him spread everywhere.

Worldwide depression everywhere,
Herb Hoover is to blame.
Disaster on earth and in air,
Herb Hoover is to blame.

Mellon drove the engine
Hoover rang the bell
Wall Street blew the whistle
And the country went to Hell.

When the twentieth century had opened, thousands of farmers, seeing only a rosy future, had saddled themselves with heavy mortgages to buy more land and more machinery. Bankers and financiers encouraged them to follow this course, but in the 1930s, both lenders and borrowers paid a price for their starry-eyed dreams. Farmers were the first victims of the Great Depression.

During the dizzying decade of the twenties, farm sectors in the nation had been allowed to stagnate and even fall backward. Instant millionaires were made on Wall Street gambles, but few seemed to care about farmers. Indeed, net farm income remained static at about 9 billion during all the years that corporate and speculative profits were zooming off the charts. The value of farm lands decreased from 80 billion to around 55 billion, and the rate of farm bankruptcies multiplied six times over. From early 1930, farm income dropped steadily. In that year it was 4.1 billion, 3.2 billion in the next, and 1.9 billion in 1932, a 50 percent drop in three years![2]

The American Communist Party, linked closely to Moscow, tried hard to win support from America's stricken farmers. The goal of communism was to make farms the collective property of the state, but that concept had almost no appeal to American men and women who still clung to ideas about self-sufficiency. Nevertheless, there were enough confrontations and violence between groups and law enforcement agencies that serious historians began to wonder if the nation might be stampeded into a state governed either by the radical right or the radical left.

In February, 1933, the State of Minnesota banned mortgage foreclosures on farms and homes. The sentiment spread to other states, and the Minnesota Act was reviewed by the U.S. Supreme Court where it was sustained by a 5 to 4 decision.[3]

Farmers had long been considered as the most conservative of citizens, yet it was in Iowa—the state with more than one-quarter of the nation's top grade soil—that sunburned men of native stock reached for pitchforks and shotguns.

In late April, 1933, the Hawkeye State teetered on the brink of anarchy. Dairymen in northwest Iowa boycotted milk creameries of Sioux City. Keeping milk from their own farms off the market so angered some Iowans that they set up road blocks to prevent anyone from delivering milk to Sioux City processors. Protesters were taking up arms against a system that paid them two cents a quart for milk that distributors in Sioux City sold for eight cents.

Farm strikers and sheriff deputies were injured in roadblock confrontations around Sioux City, Des Moines, Council Bluffs, Clinton, and other towns in the

Hawkeye State. Near Cherokee, Iowa, fourteen strikers were wounded when nine masked men opened fire and threw tear gas bombs into their camp. A South Dakota man was mortally wounded when he tried to move a truckload of milk past the blockade in Sioux City, and a deputy sheriff at Council Bluffs was killed when a riot gun was accidentally fired.

In late April, 1933, dozens of farmers wandered into the O'Brien County Courthouse in northwestern Iowa, where, on the third floor, a sheriff was scheduled to sell the land of a farmer unable to keep up his mortgage payments. On the second floor, twenty sheriff deputies armed with axe handles stood ready, prepared to deal with troublemakers. Irate farmers rushed the deputies, but in the bloody fight the deputies won out and the farmers were repulsed.

Angrier still, and abetted by swigs of homemade liquor, the mob of farmers moved toward LeMars, a town of 8,000 twenty-five miles northeast of Sioux City. In a courtroom there, District Judge C. C. Bradley was conducting a hearing on another farm foreclosure. The mob had swelled to about 100 persons, and as it pushed into the court, chambers members refused to take off their hats or snub their cigarettes. Judge Bradley banged his gavel and called for respect of the law, but his call only fueled more anger in the dozen or more men who swarmed to the bench, grabbed the judge, and demanded a promise that he would sign no more farm foreclosures.

Sixty-three years later an Iowa newspaper gave a graphic account of what happened next:

The judge trembled and the color drained from his face. But he would not give in to the mob's demands. The men who had gathered around him began slapping and hitting him. Bradley was blindfolded, led from the courthouse, put in a truck, and driven out of town. Encircled by his tormentors, Bradley was crowned with a greasy hubcap. A rope was tossed over a telephone-line crossbar and a noose draped around his neck.

Men began to hoist him into the air. But still he would not give in to the mob's demands.

Bradley fainted and slumped to the ground. The mob, frightened by its own murderous potential, broke up and ran. Bradley was shaken but not badly hurt. [4]

The effects of the nationwide economic depression begun in 1929 were slowly cumulative, and it was December of 1930 before their full force was evident. By then, commodity and wholesale prices had declined sharply; foreign trade had fallen off more than 25 percent; there was less spending, and money went into hiding; factories shut their doors; failures grew, and wage-cutting and lay-offs had become common.

During fall and winter of 1930, almost every industrial center in the country had huge lines of hungry, jobless men and women.. Commodity prices dropped 18 percent as compared with the previous year; the price of wheat plummeted by 45 percent, cotton likewise. Copper fell 47 percent, rubber 55 percent, and silver bullion 32 percent. Car loadings declined by 13 percent, steel production by 27 percent, and automobile production by 40 percent. The focus of the infection was the New York Stock Exchange.

The volume of trading on the Exchange (i.e. the total number of shares bought and sold) had risen by a series of unprecedented leaps from 451 million dollars in 1926 to 1.1 billion in 1929. A huge proportion of the trading, possibly a third or more, was done on margin, meaning that a broker asked for only about 10 or 20 percent down payment by the customer on a block of stock. In effect, the broker was loaning the buyer the remaining portion of the purchase price.

After the market crash of 1929, brokers could no longer afford to make such loans. By November of that fateful year, brokers were calling for higher margin payments, cash, or securities from buyers; customers unable to comply lost all they had ventured.

In actions often based on rumor, queues to withdraw deposits started forming outside perfectly sound banks. Any run on a bank forced it to close its doors. The worst bank failure in American history was that of the Bank of the United States on December 11, 1930, nine days after President Herbert Hoover had stated in a message to Congress, "The fundamental strength of the Nation's economy is unimpaired."

Despite Hoover's assurance, ranks of the unemployed kept skyrocketing. The Department of Labor estimated that at the beginning of 1931 more than four and a half million workers were idle. Bread lines lengthened and soup kitchens bulged as hungry citizens lined up for a few morsels. From urban centers, thousands of jobless families moved to farms or villages where they could survive on semi-subsistence levels. When ever-expanding relief rolls reached eighteen million men, women, and children, urban police chiefs worried about possible violence.

The entire economy was snowballing downhill. Citizens, leery of banks, stashed currency in safe-deposit boxes and mattresses; consumer buying fell to unprecedented lows, and every kind of business suffered. Employees were discharged and, unable to find other jobs, defaulted on mortgages or loan payments, while spending their meager savings just to stay alive. Factory payrolls dropped to less than half those of early 1929. Over city dumps, jobless men and women picked through debris, hoping to find something of value.

As the year closed, the number of unemployed was estimated variously at 5,000,000 to 7,000,000 persons, and the Bureau of Labor Statistics announced that pay rolls were 40 percent lower than in 1825.[5]

Chapter 3: Daily Lives

Soon after the turn of the century, when young men started looking for jobs in Ohio and other parts of the Midwest, they learned there was little for them but a life of laboring for someone else. The opportunities were farther west in the Texas Panhandle or in newly-opened lands of Oklahoma. Thousands heeded the advice and went west to homestead in northern plains where people were rushing to take the gamble. At first, it paid off handsomely.

Growth in the manufacturing of automobiles led to off-springs like trucks and tractors. Motor trucks became formidable rivals for railroads, and as tractors were made available to farmers, Midwestern prairies and western grasslands—formerly range areas—were plowed and seeded for ever larger crops of wheat.

By the close of the 1920s, most of the land granted to aspiring farmers under the first Homestead Act of 1862 and the later Enlarged Homestead Act of 1909 was down to the ugliest dirt in the panhandles of Texas and Oklahoma. Newspapers, books, and movies later would tell of terrible dust storms and the trek of "Okie" families going toward the promise of California. Indeed, living conditions in eastern and central Oklahoma and Kansas were bad, but farther west in the panhandles of those two states they were truly deplorable.

Nearly half the land in the panhandle areas was considered only marginal for farming; nevertheless, people whose kin had been serfs, sharecroppers, tenants, and even slaves or castaways wanted to own a piece of earth. The name *Oklahoma* came from a combination of two Choctaw words—*okla,* which meant people, and *humma* the word for red—land which first raised cattle, then wheat, and at last gushed oil, a land which turned dirt farmers into millionaires or paupers.[1]

The Wall Street gyrations of 1929 were slow to hit the High Plains of Texas and Oklahoma. The 1928 wheat crop had come in as usual with the price holding at about $1.00 per bushel. Most people had anticipated $1.50 and some even had hoped for $2.00, the price they had got at the start of the decade, but it was not to be. A hundred years earlier, it had taken fifty-eight hours of labor to plant and harvest a single acre of wheat; the tractor changed everything. A tractor could do the work of ten horses, and with combines a farmer could cut and thresh the grain in one swoop. By 1930, every wheat farmer had to have a tractor, a combine, and a one-way plow—the latter vehicle, cursed in future decades as the tool that destroyed the plains and ripped up the grass, seemed a godsend to hard-working farmers.

The wheat crop of 1930 was a bumper, the price a disaster. Wheat sat in elevators, in piles, or moldered on the ground. There was so much grain in Iowa and Nebraska that people burned it for fuel; one courthouse kept its furnaces going all winter on surplus corn. In southwest Kansas, the crop was up 50 percent above the previous year, and in the county around Dalhart, Texas, it was up 100 percent.[2]

At the start of that year, a bushel of wheat sold for less than one-eighth of the high price from ten years earlier. Forty cents per bushel would barely cover costs, let alone pay any interest on the bank loan. Most growers thought their salvation lay in planting more wheat, so they plowed up what grass remained, ripped out more sod, and hoped to have another large crop when prices came back.

Statistics of the decade of the thirties revealed that the nation's population increase of only 7.2 percent in ten years was less than half of any previous decade. Marriages during the depression years were few and long deferred—the lowest marriage rate in the history of the nation. A legal divorce was looked at with askance—often becoming a local scandal, and throughout the leanest years of the thirties, many couples opted for desertion, the "poor man's divorce." In 1916, the year before the U.S. entered the First World War, births among American citizenry had occurred at the rate of 25 per 1,000; by 1929 the figure had declined to 18.9 percent, and by 1933 had fallen even further—to 16.6 percent, rising only slightly during the decade.[3]

Birth control and deferred marriages were reflected in the size of the family. At the turn of the century, the American home had an average of three children; by 1939 there were only one or two.

The 1930s demanded physical labor, particularly on farms, villages, and small towns. Truck farmers and share croppers could nearly always be found eking out existences in the Midwest and on outskirts of bigger cities. The central and northern regions of Indiana and Illinois were examples.

Onions and potatoes were the dominant crops on the truck farms, but other vegetables also were raised. In onion farming, seeds were drilled during the last week of March or first of April. The chosen land most likely would be "muck"—a peat-like soil. The "muck" consisted of light grains or fragments of organic deposits and, therefore, needed no fertilizers. Unfortunately, like Irish peat, the muck of Indiana and Illinois could burn; fires underground would smolder for years. Moreover, the light, porous muck soil often was blown away by high winds in spring and summer.

The workday on truck farms was ten hours—from 7 in the morning until 12 noon—lunch under a shaded tree, then back to the field from 12:30 to 5:30 P.M. Weeders crawling the fields were barefooted, bonneted with straw hats, and boys and men were usually shirtless if they tanned easily. Muck under a July or August sun could get so hot it seemed to burn the hands and knees, but an inch below it could be cooler. The work was tiring, and most weeders leaned on one hand, using the other one for thumbing out the tiny, emerging, pesky, unwanted growths.

A fourteen or fifteen-year-old boy might be paid 15 cents or even 20 cents per hour for weeding, and during harvesting could top 40 to 50 crates of yellow, large, Sweet Spanish onions. At 15 cents per hour for weeding and at .03 cents per crate for topping, he would work in the field for ten hours each day. His wages would give him enough to take his best girl to two different movies and enjoy popcorn and a coke with her on each occasion

A railroad boxcar held 500 fifty-pound bags of onions—an average yield for one acre of yellows. In Chicago, Indianapolis, and Terre Haute markets during the mid-1930s, each fifty-pound bag would bring at most $1.08 .

Cabbages, cucumbers, tomatoes, turnips, and carrots also were raised and marketed by truck farmers and share croppers. The processes differed according to the vegetable, but planting, tending, harvesting, and marketing each of them called for physical labor, long hours, and low wages.

In bad times, the whole family suffers, but the plight of women during the Great Depression of the 1930s was almost unendurable. "Man works from dawn to setting sun, but woman's work is never done," said the adage. Washing, ironing, house cleaning, canning, cooking, mending, occasional quilting bees, Saturday night in town, and church on Sundays, followed by a huge family dinner. These were the parameters of life for most rural women in 1930.

Although the Nineteenth Amendment, ratified in August of 1920, had granted them the right to vote, the status of women in society had not changed much since the days of the Civil War. A few might become school teachers, office workers, or underpaid store clerks, but most would end up as wives and mothers consigned to lifetimes of drudgery and hours of caring for husbands and children.

In the hinterlands, Monday was wash day—no exceptions. Water was heated in a boiler, often copper of the kind that in later years might be polished and used for flower beds or magazine holders. After water in the boiler was heated, it was poured into a tub with soap added, either Proctor & Gamble or homemade, and the wash begun. Taking one piece at a time, whoever was doing the washing would rub the soaked article against a "washboard"—a two by four contraption with metal corrugated surfaces. Then the piece was ready for rinsing in another tub of clean water. After that came the wringing, during which the person would feed the rinsed article piece by piece through hand-operated rollers. Next, hung on a clothesline strung across the yard, the washed pieces would dry in sunshine or wind before being folded for ironing the next day.

On farms and in small towns, the kitchen was the home's heart, and there a stove was its driving force. There was no living in a house until its kitchen range was set up and stoked. The kitchen range was used for heat, cooking, water reservoir, and for drying wet mittens or soggy overshoes. Across the top of the stove would be six cooking lids which required no blacking, and below them was a twenty-inch square, steel lined, cast iron oven with a door boasting a dialed heat register. On one side of this kitchen monarch was the fire box, built over a grate, the shaking of which each morning marked the start of a new day. The fire box could take either wood or coal, and on its opposite side would be the water reservoir, where contents were kept warm by nearby heat. Corn cobs were the most likely kindling; sticks and twigs were slower to start but could be used if cobs had not been gathered. No small wonder that life revolved around the kitchen stove.[4]

In cities, the jobless were the most conspicuous feature of the dismal landscape during Depression years. Men gathered in poolrooms and taverns, sat on benches in the park when the weather was fair—often slept there at night, too—huddled in empty doorways when it rained, or joined companions in clubrooms of the Elks, Odd Fellows, or Kiwanis.

Transients rode the rails. Singly or in groups, men who had no work sneaked into boxcars and drifted from town to town with no hope beyond something to eat or pick up a dollar chopping wood, pushing a wheelbarrow, harvesting a crop, washing dishes—anything for a buck.

Many in this population of floaters were veterans of the Bonus Expeditionary Force—the ragged army of some 25,000 WWI veterans who converged in Washington in June 1932 to try to pressure Congress into passing legislation to pay them a cash bonus for their military service.

In the late spring and summer of 1932, and in the spirit of Coxey's Army*, eleven thousand men—many of them with families—arrived in Washington, D.C. In preceding years, the American Legion had campaigned for a "bonus" payment to veterans of World War I.

President Hoover, like Harding before him and Franklin Roosevelt following him, opposed veterans' subsidies beyond those already in effect. The three executives argued that the payment would cost the government 1.7 billion, with a large portion of it going to veterans who needed no relief.

Douglas MacArthur had been appointed Chief of Staff for the American Army in November, 1930, and in that role was in command of forces charged with protecting the Capitol. Some protesters settled in shantytowns outside the city; others occupied vacant federal buildings on Pennsylvania Avenue, and still more milled around the Capitol. A later survey would show that 94 percent of them had army or navy records; 67 percent had served overseas, and 20 percent had been disabled. General MacArthur refused to believe such reports and was convinced that 90 percent of the protesters were fakers.

Federal investigators charged that Communists had captured leadership of the bonus marchers. When efforts of the District of Columbia's police to remove the marchers failed, President Hoover was asked for Army assistance. He ordered General MacArthur to complete an evacuation of protestors around the Capitol. No one was killed in the ensuing confrontations, though many were injured in the stampede that resulted when U. S. cavalrymen, led by MacArthur, surged into the crowd.[5]

A dozen and a half years later, General Courtney Whitney, one of MacArthur's most fervent aides, wrote that bonus marchers' ranks were filled with a "heavy

---

* In 1894 Jacob Sechler Coxey of Pennsylvania and Ohio led a march of more than 100 men into Washington, D.C. where he and other leaders of the "Army" were arrested for walking on the Capitol lawn.

---

percentage of criminals, men with prison records for such crimes as murder, manslaughter, rape, robbery, burglary, blackmail, and assault."

Whitney asserted further:

A secret document which was captured later disclosed that the Communist plan covered even such details as the public trial and hanging in the front of the Capitol of high government officials. At the very top of the list was the name of Army Chief of Staff Douglas MacArthur.[6]

Throughout most of the 1920s, the mood of America was euphoric; most believed the four horsemen of the Apocalypse had been banished forever. The nation was thriving, but prosperity was not to last. Looking backwards, economists and historians disagree over whether the stock market crash started the Great Depression or whether the Depression spawned the debacle. Although cause of the gloomy era may be uncertain, its aspects are indisputable.

CHAPTER 4: A MOBILE SOCIETY

Gasoline motors sped up movement of the nation's population from east to farther west. Citizens followed journalist Horace Greeley's admonition, "Go west young man! Go west!" Little did it matter that when Greeley tendered his advice, by "west" he had meant Erie County, Pennsylvania.

Westward migration had been well underway by the opening of the 1930s. Better roads, more trains and automobiles, available land sweetened by various Homestead Acts created by the federal government, along with undaunted courage and adventurous spirits in the characters of many families—these and other factors had combined to encourage movement west. The urban movement was stronger even than the westward movement.

Statistics showed that for every state except Maine, New Hampshire, Vermont, Rhode Island, Pennsylvania, Georgia, Arkansas, and Utah, the average number of persons per farm was less in 1935 than in 1930. In 1935 the average number of persons per farm was 4.67 as compared with 4.84 five years earlier in 1930.

The factory system for cotton spinning and weaving remained in New England states, as did manufacturing of woolen blankets, clothes, boots, and shoes. Most small factories relied on water power rather than bituminous coal, plentiful in the area. It was said that nearly every waterfall in Connecticut, for example, was harnessed to a small factory turning out machine tools, firearms, furniture, clocks, and other oddments. Young couples on farms and villages, looking at six-and-a-half-day work weeks for ten or more hours of labor each day, wanted to taste the delights of metropolis, such as New York, Chicago, Dallas, Los Angeles, and San Francisco. Trains, automobiles, telephones, radios, and popular magazines let the boy or girl in Bean Blossom, Kansas, or Pumpkin Creek, Indiana, follow the lives of persons who strolled Broadway, made moving picture shows in Hollywood, or rode the trolley cars in San Francisco. Those places were where the glamour was.

Just a few years before the beginning of the twentieth century, entrepreneurs discovered that if you could sell magazines to enough people you could sell them for less than the cost of their production. The secret was to attract advertisers who would pay hefty sums for inclusion of promotional notices. Like Harriet Beecher

Stowe's "Topsy," the business of national advertising just "growed."

The rise of the advertising credo can be shown in revenues of one of the most popular weeklies—the *Saturday Evening Post*. In 1902, that magazine sold 314,671 copies per issue, and brought in $360,125 in revenue from advertising. Twenty years later, in 1922, it was selling 2,187,024 copies per issue—almost seven times as many as in 1902—while its advertising earnings soared to $28,278,755, more than 78 times as much as in 1902.[1]

Advertising whetted America's hunger for bigness in everything, from trains to automobiles, and from individually run "Mom and Pop" stores to huge corporate ownerships. Bankers lent enough capital to form businesses whose enterprises spread from coast to coast, building in cities of any size department stores which looked like palaces. Chain stores were on their way, led by Woolworth's five-and-ten and by A & P stores which in 1912 had opened in Newark on a cash-and-carry basis. The rise of chain stores gave more evidence of the logic of mass production: if you built enough of your product, you could attract millions of buyers, you could cut your prices way down by the placement of huge bulk orders, and you'd still reap profits galore.

In 1908, forty-five-year-old Detroiter Henry Ford had wanted to manufacture an automobile not for the wealthy but for ordinary wage-earners. Soon afterwards he came out with a four-wheeled vehicle he called the Model T. He believed that if he concentrated on a single model, he could cut the cost of manufacturing to the point where common citizens could afford it.

Accordingly, as his sales increased, he reduced his product's price still further and by 1913 had installed his cost-cutting principle of assembly line production. Responding to interviewers, he said, "A customer can have a car painted any color he wants as long as it is black."

At the opening of the decade in 1930, most automobiles on American roads were made by Henry Ford, and jokes about his "Tin Lizzies" were as likely to be thrown into casual conversation as talk about weather, crops, or politics. Some samples:

One man on his deathbed had a final request to make—that his Model T be buried with him because he "had never been in a hole yet that his Ford couldn't get him out."

Another that went around said, "The guy who owns a Model T might not have a quarrelsome disposition, but he's always trying to start something."

And there was this one:
"Have you heard the last Ford story?"
"I hope so."

The craving for autos was best shown in everyday expressions. In Muncie, Indiana, one woman, mother of nine children, answered an investigator's question by saying, "We'd rather do without clothes than give up the car." Another commented on the fact that her family owned a car but no bathtub. "Why," she explained, "you can't go to town in a bathtub."[2]

Ford was not without competition, for hundreds of gadget-minded men—bicycle makers, wagon builders, axle manufacturers, mechanics, and entrepreneurs of all sorts—rushed to make the new vehicles. Names like Locomobile, Owen Magnetic, Franklin, Pierce-Arrow, Apperson, and Briscoe flourished for a short time before collapsing. Some of their patents and ideas were transmitted to survivors like Studebaker, Chrysler, and a giant New Jersey holding company growing from Buick Motors. Founder of the new company was William C. Durant—a promoter who called his venture General Motors.

Henry Ford's genius showed itself in making automobiles more popular and affordable to average citizens. Manufacturers learned to turn out cars with prices low enough to attract blue-collar workers. By the late 1920s, most U.S. auto plants were producing vehicles with windows that could be closed to keep out dust or rain. With such improvements, a man could take his family out for an afternoon drive in the countryside or even visit friends or relatives forty or fifty miles away.

In 1920 there had been slightly more than 8 million cars registered in the United States; by 1925 the number had nearly doubled, and by the beginning of 1930 it had reached over 23 million.[3] Parallel with improved means of production came the practice of installment selling of automobiles. At the time of WWI, virtually all autos were sold for cash or traded for real estate. By the mid 1920s, more than three-quarters of all cars sold, old and new, were sold on installments.

The impact of social changes brought about by more widespread ownership of autos was rapid and far-reaching. Suburbs which had been small and accessible only by horse and buggy or trains grew with startling speeds. From these communities, a family wage-earner in his auto could drive to his place of work. Roads, formerly dusty, muddy, and unmapped, were improved, hardened, often MacAdamized, or even paved by concrete. Highways were numbered, given banked curves, and along the popular routes, motor inns and cabins began to appear. The downtown hotel on Main Street, where every traveling salesman coming into town used to stay, lost business to the tourist camp out on the highway.

In 1930, when the country's total population stood at 123 million, the nation could boast of 26 and one-half million registered vehicles, 74 percent of the world's total. Eight years later, the number of registered vehicles had risen three million, 68 percent of the world's total.[4]

In the formative years of the American Republic, tariffs had been used mainly to provide revenue, but as the nation grew, advocates in various administrations, despite arguments from free trade promoters, imposed levies for strengthening domestic industries against foreign competition. The Smoot-Hawley Tariff of June, 1931, for example, raised rates on agricultural raw materials from 38 percent to 49 percent and on other commodities from 31 percent to 34 percent, with special protection given to sugar and textile interests.

In the early 1930s, when the economy worsened, farmers were hit especially hard. A farmer is an independent individual and normally conservative in politics. The rank-and-file farmer—brought up as a conservative and voting the straight ticket from McKinley to Hoover—is honorable and wants to pay his debts. Prior to 1932 when crops failed, prices dropped, or weather turned sour, there wasn't much for him to do but "slop the hogs and damn the Democrats." In Iowa, heart of the corn country, it was commonly observed that "if our state ever goes Democratic, Hell will go Methodist."

With the coming of the black horse in the early thirties, farm incomes toppled like dominoes—a fifty percent drop in less than three years—and farm debt increased in reverse ratio to the decline in income; thousands of farm families were forced off the land either by foreclosure or destitution. Average farm family income, which had been about $2,300 in 1929, fell to less than $1600 or less in 1932.[5]

Such economic woes made American farmers desperate. A farmer wouldn't buy hay, seed, or livestock from a neighbor because most likely whatever payment could be made would go to a creditor. First, creditors would take the farm, then the livestock, and next the farm machinery. Finally, they'd have a sale for household goods, but such sales seldom paid all the debts. Sometimes sympathetic neighbors united and came *en masse* to an auction, where they crowded out other prospective buyers before bidding a penny themselves, buying the item, and then giving it back to the owner.

County courthouses burned corn; it was cheaper than coal. Oscar Heline, who lived in the northwestern part of Iowa, described the practice:

A county just east of here, they burned corn in their courthouse all winter, '32, '33. You couldn't hardly buy groceries for corn. It couldn't pay the transportation. In South Dakota, the county elevator listed corn as minus three cents. Minus three cents a bushel. If you wanted to sell 'em a bushel of corn, you had to bring in three cents. They couldn't afford to handle it. Just think of what happens when you can't get out from under.[6]

CHAPTER 5: FRINGE ELEMENTS

As bad as conditions were in the hinterlands, misery in cities was worse—so bad that many citizens tried to escape back to farms or villages where they hoped living costs would be less and they could grow their own food. For countless thousands, however, escapes were impossible. In metropolitan centers like New York City, Chicago, St. Louis, San Francisco, and others, unemployment skyrocketed.

At the beginning of 1931, President Hoover's Department of Labor estimated that four and a half million citizens were without jobs. On city corners, jobless men sold apples for a nickel or dime apiece; soup kitchens and bread lines were set up to feed the hungry, and eventually relief rolls swelled to more than eighteen million men, women, and children. The worst of the disaster came in 1932 when the full impact of Europe's shattered economy reached America.

Relief agencies stretched their meager budgets to the limits. Some agencies provided only food, and no money for rent, electricity, gas, or medical services. New York City paid $2.39 a week to take care of an entire family,

Democrats in 1930 put the entire blame for the Depression on Hoover, Coolidge, and Harding. Their appeal won voters, and in congressional elections that year, Democrats captured the House by a margin of five seats and dominated the Senate by allying themselves with progressive Republicans. Democrat John Nance Garner, Texan and Speaker of the House, began planning political strategy for the election two years away. Meanwhile, President Hoover would be the devil.

Born in 1874 to a farming couple in West Branch, Iowa, Herbert Clark Hoover, called Bertie as a boy, was one of the world's greatest humanitarians in the period of WWI, and for four years (1929-1933) was the thirty-first President of the United States. Hoover's name, however, became etched in the minds of the public and in those of most historians as a failed American president, a cold man, indifferent to the country's sufferings. Not until after the Second World War did Hoover and his record get a closer look.

Orphaned at ten or eleven years old, Hoover had grown up with relatives in Oklahoma, Iowa, Oregon, and California. Although impoverished, he was able to attend Stanford University, working his way through that school, and secured a degree in geology. In his geology lab, he met a student named Lou Henry and discovered she, too, had come originally from Iowa.

At first it seemed only a friendship, and upon graduation Bert Hoover became a mining engineer, sent to various regions of the world. His job was to explore, examine business records, and report on the conditions of gold, tin, and other mines in Southeast Asia. His diligent work, talents, and business acumen prompted him to invest in a few of the failed mines. He and Lou Henry were keeping in touch by mail, but unfortunately, none of those letters has ever been discovered. Both proved to be very private persons.

It was not until 1899, when both Bert Hoover and Lou Henry were twenty-five years old, that he had saved enough money for them to marry. Actually, he had made and saved far more than almost any of couples marrying at the turn of that century. His expert judgments and saving habits had made him almost a millionaire within five years of his graduation from college.

In 1914, when WWI began, Hoover, his wife Lou, and their two small sons were living in London. Belgium almost immediately declared its neutrality, but it stood in the way of the impending German attack on France. The Belgian army fought valiantly and slowed but failed to halt German advances. Grain harvests in Belgium were decimated, and the few crops reaped were confiscated by the Kaiser's armies. In the years before WWI, Belgium had imported large quantities of food but, hemmed in by British blockades during that war, was unable to do so. Without outside assistance, the entire population faced hunger and mass starvation.

In London, Herbert Hoover devised a plan that would feed the entire Belgian nation from 1914 until 1920. An international commission was created and named the Committee for Relief of Belgium with Hoover at its head. Under his spur, sponsors raised huge amounts of money from French, British, and American governments as well as through private fund-raising campaigns. One biographer estimated that through Hoover's efforts and the commission, more than 200 million was collected, 24 million which was spent on reconstruction at the war's end. In the years of its existence, the Committee for Relief saved more than nine million Belgians from starvation.[1]

Hoover held no public office at the end of WWI, but he emerged from it recognized as the Great Humanitarian. He had registered as a Republican and had supported Theodore Roosevelt's run on the Bull Moose ticket in 1912. As the presidential race heated up in 1920, he was courted by both political parties in America but disavowed any active interest in campaigning, withdrawing his name from presidential primaries wherever possible. In Michigan, that was not permissible, and enthusiasts there placed his name on both Republican and Democratic ballots. That year the Republican nod went to Senator Warren G. Harding of Ohio, who went on to defeat soundly the Democratic team of James Cox, also from Ohio, and his running mate, Franklin D. Roosevelt of New York.

Hoover joined the Harding administration as Secretary of Commerce, and in that post he again displayed the talents and zeal that had been so successful in the past. His enthusiasms expanded the Commerce Department so much that a quip around Washington was "Hoover is Secretary of Commerce and undersecretary of everything else."

President Harding died in August, 1923, and was succeeded in office by Calvin Coolidge of Vermont. Hoover continued to serve as Secretary of Commerce although under the budget-minded Coolidge his latitude was more restricted. In 1927, Coolidge startled presidential watchers with his cryptic announcement: "I do not choose to run for President in 1928."

Republicans held their 1928 convention in Kansas City, and there Herbert Hoover met with little opposition. He was nominated on the first ballot, as was Charles Curtis for the Vice-Presidency. The Democrats met in Houston, Texas, and chose Alfred E. Smith for the top position with Senator Joe Robinson of Arkansas for the vice presidency.

Presidential campaigns that year were exciting. Republicans praised the Coolidge administrations, lauded protectionism, gave approval to none of the Congressional panaceas for farm relief, and, regarding Prohibition, promised continued "vigorous enforcement." Democrats advanced no specific programs; they straddled tariff questions insisting, however, that their program would "maintain legitimate business and a high standard of wages."

Smith mounted a gallant fight, but odds were against him. He was strictly urbanite, a Catholic, and had little to offer either labor or agriculture. An even greater handicap grew from the fact that he was a "wet" as far as Prohibition was concerned.

Poll results in November showed an overwhelming victory for Hoover and the Republicans. The former Quaker, mining expert, millionaire, and Secretary of Commerce won 444 electoral votes compared with only 87 for his opponent. Popular votes for Hoover were 21,392,000 and 15,016,000 for Smith.[2]

Hoover brought with him into the White House the views that had made him successful in the business world. A firm believer in individualism and American industrialism, he opposed any sort of political or social change that might smell of socialism. He envisioned an America in which factory wheels turned incessantly, working men were always employed with wages enabling them to buy more automobiles, radios, and electrical appliances—trappings of a good life.

Before the first half of his administration was over, President Hoover began tasting the bitter dregs of defeat. Politicians were demanding legislation for their local bailiwicks; businessmen clamored for support and more tariff protection; and the whole capitalistic world—one which he had regarded as inexorable—simply collapsed. Where prosperity once had been everywhere, by 1930 it had been replaced by destitution and poverty.

Moreover, the Great Humanitarian was opposed by a hostile Congress in nearly everything he tried. In the Senate, Norris of Nebraska led an insurgent bloc canceling the President on his tariff, waterpower, and farm relief programs. One result was the writing and the signing by the President of the Tariff Act of 1930, with the highest schedules of rates that protectionists had yet gained.

By the end of October, 1929, Herbert Clark Hoover had been in the presidency for eight months. When the first signs of economic troubles appeared, he had summoned business executives to Washington and had assured them that "business conditions were fundamentally sound." There would be no wage cutting; that measure wouldn't work. He believed and remained convinced that the financial panic raging in Europe was the cause of market disturbances in America.

In January 1932, Hoover—the lame duck president—persuaded Congress to create the Reconstruction Finance Corporation, capitalized at $2 billion, and to set it up as a "bankers' bank." The goal of the RFC was to bring federal aid to hard-pressed banks, and its entrance into a community, as well as saving business enterprises, often brought all the excitement of a fire brigade. The rate of failure for individual banks during the RFC's first year of operation was cut by almost a third. Yet, despite success of the RFC, Hoover remained adamant about interfering with normal business practices: the best way was for government to stand aside and let buyers and sellers in the open market determine the management of business and industry.

In 1932, when active campaigning for the presidency got underway, the Depression was in the middle of its third year. There was no question of President Hoover's re-nomination, but the Republican Party and its leader had lost support from the electorate.

Democrats nominated Governor Franklin Roosevelt of New York for the presidency and chose John Nance Garner of Texas for the vice presidency. Roosevelt's energetic campaigning electrified the country, and voters went to the polls that fall to repudiate overwhelmingly President Hoover and his conservative outlook.

Years later after having broken with New Dealers, the outspoken Garner said, "I fought President Hoover with everything I had under Marquis of Queensberry, London, prize ring, and catch-as-catch-can rules." Yet Garner added that he thought Hoover "the wisest statesman" on world affairs and perhaps upon domestic problems also.[3]

At the time of the market crash, men who later would gain national or even international fame were not well known. Hard times brought out all kinds of suggested remedies—everything from adjustment and repairs to complete overthrow. One panacea offered by Francis Everett Townsend won the hearts of *geriatric* voters—*geriatrics,* a word not in most dictionaries of the time.

Townsend had graduated from The University of Nebraska Medical School and had practiced his profession in Long Beach, California. In 1933, when America was mired in the lowest depths of the Depression, Townsend advocated an old-age pension plan, which called for a stipend of $200 each month to be issued to all citizens 60 years of age or older. Funds for the program were to be raised by a 2 percent federal sales tax, and a condition of the grant was that each recipient had to spend the $200 in the U.S. within a month of its receipt. The simplicity of Townsend's proposal and his zeal in promoting it attracted huge numbers of citizens who formed nationwide pressure groups.

Despite its condemnation by most recognized economists, Townsendites garnered enough support to get several bills introduced on the floor of the U.S. Congress. Each bill was defeated, and by 1935, when employment began moving upward again and Social Security became a new law, the spread and vigor of the Townsend Plan declined and fell into the dustbin of lost causes.

Another calamity howler of the Depression Era was Charles Edward Coughlin, a Roman Catholic priest ordained in 1916. Ten years after his ordainment, he was appointed pastor of the Shrine of the Little Flower at Royal Oak, Michigan. Coughlin had a fine speaking voice for radio, and over that medium he first supported Franklin Roosevelt; then in 1934, he began breaking away from the New Deal. Throwing aside his earlier allegiance, Coughlin broadcast increasingly bitter attacks against FDR and the administration.

The most obvious break came in the middle of January, 1935, when President Roosevelt sent to Congress a special message calling for U.S. entrance into the World Court. As expected, isolationists in the Senate led by Hiram Johnson of California and William Borah of Idaho attacked the proposal and were joined by Senator Huey Long of Louisiana, who had begun challenging FDR for the party's fervor.

On Sunday afternoons, Father Coughlin in his radio addresses jumped into the fray. For several weeks in radio talks, Coughlin surpassed even Huey Long as the most influential spokesman against FDR. Coughlin, in his rich, deep, melodious, intimately confiding voice—"one of the great speaking voices of the twentieth century . . . a voice made for promises"—a voice perfectly suited to the lush rhetoric it intoned, the Radio Priest warned audiences and readers that the Republic was in mortal danger, the Senate was about to sacrifice "our national sovereignty to the World Court" at the behest of an administration "ready to join hands" with those wicked international bankers—the Rothschilds, Morgans, Warburgs, Kuhns, and Loebs—who had tricked us into a bloody European war in 1917 and were trying to do so again.[4]

Coughlin founded a weekly paper he called *Social Justice*, and he used it to reinforce whatever preachments he made over the radio. It was speculated that Coughlin's true goal was to launch a third party, for he likened the two major ones as twin thieves. In early May 1935, Father Coughlin's people attempted to build a larger base and sought support from proponents of Dr. Townsend and Gerald L. K. Smith, a budding fascist who led an assortment of rabble-rousers.

Smith had adopted the views of Huey Long from Louisiana, and may even have been a greater spellbinder than Huey himself. On the platform, Smith's mighty voice could be heard for blocks as he trumpeted under such slogans as Share Our Wealth, picked up from Long's preachments. H. L. Mencken, cynic from Baltimore, judged that as an orator Gerald Smith was more impressive than the god-like Wm. Jennings Bryan. Regarding Smith, Mencken wrote,

Throw together a flashing eye, a hairy chest, a rubescent complexion, large fists, a voice both loud and mellow, terrifying and reassuring, sforzando *and* pizzicato, *and finally, an unearthly capacity for distending the superficial blood vessels of his temples and neck, as if they were biceps—and you have the makings of a boob-bumper worth going miles to see.*[5]

Although capable of sending supporters into wild passions, neither Father Coughlin from Detroit nor Dr. Townsend from California aroused the nation's malcontents to heights achieved by Huey Pierce Long—a man from the Deep South.

The Seventy-Third Session of the U.S. Congress opened in January, 1932, and among its newly-elected members stood Huey P. Long, Democratic senator from the State of Louisiana. He had risen from the swamps of Louisiana, where radicalism flourished along with alligators, water moccasins, and fevers. The seventh of nine children, Huey as a youth was used to hard work and later said, "I hated the farm work . . . . Rising before the sun, we toiled until dark."

Habits of work and determination carried over into Long's young manhood, and in 1913, during his stint as an itinerant drummer for kitchen utensils, he married a girl who won a cooking contest he himself sponsored. His bride urged him to get more education, and they were able to save enough for Long to enter the law school at Tulane University. Studying from sixteen to eighteen hours a day, he completed a three-year law course in eight months and then talked the Chief Justice of the State into giving him a special bar examination. Passing that exam, Long was admitted to the Louisiana bar in May of 1915.

At home and in daily associations, politics and religion—both revivalist in style—were Huey's stock in trade. His talk abounded with idioms, phrases, and anecdotes used also when he was huckstering kitchen utensils. On platforms throughout the state, he gained recognition as a radical populist, and his loquacity won him the soubriquet of "Kingfish." Elected to the Governorship of Louisiana in 1928, he served in that role until 1932. As Governor, Long was an efficient administrator, sure in detail, and quick in decisions.

Long backed FDR in the election of 1932, but early in the next year, from his seat in the U.S. Senate, he broke away from the New Deal Administration and talked incessantly about the need for redistribution of the nation's wealth. In the Senate, he drafted a resolution for the Share-the-Wealth idea, but Senator Joe Robinson, Democratic leader, refused to back it. Senator Long dramatically resigned from his committee assignments and called for new leaders. Most observers saw his move as a forthcoming challenge to FDR for leadership of the Democratic Party.

Meanwhile, Long consolidated control over politics and patronage in his home state. In a series of special sessions in 1934 and 1935, his lieutenants carried out dictums to pass legislation transferring nearly every vestige of authority from towns and parishes to the state, which meant in effect Huey Long. By 1935, local government in Louisiana was virtually at an end, yet people in the state had improvements only dreamt of by their forebears. Schools, hospitals, roads, and public services were better than ever. Impoverished whites and Negroes were given great new opportunities. Long took special pride for what he had done for education, free textbooks and school busses in the elementary schools and to the new state university with its medical school at Baton Rouge.

Despite Long's visible achievements, few doubted the corruption within his regime. From his seat in the U.S. Senate, Long viewed the unequal distribution of wealth as cause for the distress and the Great Depression. He first proposed a bill in which the federal government could take by taxation all income over $1 million and all inheritances over $5 million. That idea got nowhere, and two years later he modified it by adding a capital levy which would reduce all fortunes to around $3 million. Next, he added provisions that would make the federal government furnish every American family with a "homestead allowance" of at least $5,000 and an annual income of $2,000, plus fringe benefits spelled out in his proposal.

While Coughlin and Townsend at least went through the motions of economic analysis, Long based his ideas on Scriptures, saying, "I never read a line of Marx or Henry George or any of them economists . . . It's all in the law of God."

The flamboyant Huey Long created the Share-the-Wealth program in 1934 with the motto "Every Man a King," proposing wealth distribution in the form of a net asset tax on large corporations and individuals of great wealth to curb the poverty and crime resulting from the Depression. Charismatic and immensely popular for his social reform programs and willingness to take forceful action, he was accused of dictatorial practices as he gained near-total control of his state's government.

Huey Long saw his movement as an alternative to both major political parties, and upon adjournment of Congress in the late summer of 1935, he left Washington, D.C. to return to Baton Rouge, headquarters of his statewide political machine. Shortly after nine o'clock in the evening, he was walking from the Capitol to the Governor's office when a young man stepped out of the shadows, pressed a .32 caliber pistol against Long's abdomen and fired. While Long moaned and clutched his side, the assailant prepared to fire again, but from bodyguards nearby, the gun was knocked out of his hand, and a volley of bullets from pistols and submachine guns riddled the assassin. He died instantly and medical examiners later would find more than thirty nine bullets in his riddled body.

The murderer was identified as a young doctor named Carl Austin Weiss, whose father-in-law, a judge, had been one of Long's targets in a bill passed by the legislature that very afternoon. For a day and a half, Long struggled for life, but it was a losing battle. On the morning of September 10, 1935, he died, still a young man, less than two weeks past his forty-second birthday.[6]

Chapter 6: Expanding Horizons

By the time the Great Depression started, the motor industry in America was not only producing more automobiles, it was also turning out increasing numbers of motor trucks and tractors. In the thirties, the former began rivaling railroads for freight transportation and the latter enabled a farmer to clear, plow, plant, and harvest many more acres than he could do with horses or mules.

Along with telephones, radios, and other means of communication, automobiles ended the isolation of many American farmers. Before the coming of autos, the goals of a well-off farmer had been to first paint the barn, then add a porch, and next to buy a piano. In the 1930s, any farmer making a profit would first opt to purchase an auto—one he could drive to church on Sundays, to the elevator when necessary, to town for picture shows, or shopping on Saturdays.

The automobile uprooted American society. Families which, before the advent of autos, rarely traveled more than a few miles from their homes, twenty at the most, obtained new-fangled vehicles which let them broaden their trips beyond the county seat or visits to the nearest doctor. Families could drive to the seashore, to the nearest lake on a holiday or a longer vacation, to a circus in a distant town, see new sights, and bring back tales to share with friends and neighbors.

Increased auto travel, though, brought more accidents, injuries, and sudden deaths. In 1922, the number of persons killed annually in automobile accidents throughout the United States was less than 15,000; eight years later in 1930 the figure had more than doubled to 32,000.

Roads had been improved, but on them drivers—particularly younger ones—learned to play "chicken." Older drivers usually were more cautious, but accidents could happen to anyone, and when they happened they were more fatal, because cars were more powerful and faster.

Some families disdained autos and chose other means of getting around. Horseback was limited to short distances and boats available only to those near waterways, so by the 1930s travel by train was an era of luxury for those who could afford it. Trains were fast and more comfortable than ever before. The New York Central Railroad's "Twentieth Century Limited," rated as one of the speediest on the tracks, clipped forty-five minutes from its New York to Chicago schedule in 1935.[1]

Snack bars, cocktail lounges, and roomy club cars made their appearance, and most important of all, air conditioning came to be standard on cross-country lines. Gleaming, streamlined, and diesel-powered monsters were given such names as Silver Meteor, Chief, Super-Chief, Sunset Limited, or Zephyr, and as they roared across America from coast to coast they gave people on farms and lonely towns a glimpse of the wealthy, awakening dreams of faraway places. Only passengers might see the curtained berths in Pullman cars, but spectators could catch sight of brightly-lit dining cars showing white tablecloths and sparkling silverware.

Notwithstanding widespread poverty, the first five years of the 1930s marked the crest of splendor for America's railroads. Modernization had been tremendous, but the cost had been high—hundreds of millions of dollars spent for upgrading. Passenger revenue spurted temporarily but failed to rise enough to offset expenditures. In 1930, the first full year of the Depression, thirty railroads had gone into receivership. By 1935, the figure reached eighty-seven, and five years afterwards a total of 108 lines were in receivership. By 1940, travel by private auto had grown steadily, and interurban bus lines were eating into the railroads' short haul business. Moreover, air travel, tiny in 1930, had doubled and redoubled within the ten-year period.

The decade of the thirties might be called the morning of air travel, for it was during those years that airplanes and persons who flew in them made headlines. Slight beginnings of travel by air had been made in the 1920s but was done then only by the very rich or celebrities. By the 1930s flying was still an uncommon mode of travel; one reason was that most people still considered it too dangerous. If emerging airlines were to win passengers away from trains, they would have to convince the public that air travel was safe.

Ellen Church was a person who helped spread the gospel of air safety. Church was a registered nurse from Iowa who was so captivated by flying that she had taken private lessons. She approached Boeing Airlines with hopes of becoming one of its pilots. Boeing executives gave her no encouragement toward that goal but one saw another possibility. He suggested placing Church or other registered nurses aboard Boeing aircraft. The tactic worked and did a great deal to allay public concern about air safety.

On May 20, 1927, Charles A. Lindbergh had left Roosevelt Field in New York and flown his monoplane, *Spirit of St. Louis,* non-stop to Le Bourget airfield in Paris thirty-and-a-half hours and thirty-six hundred and ten miles away. In 1938, eleven years after Lindbergh's historic flight, another flier did almost the same.

Douglas Corrigan, nicknamed "Wrong Way" and one of the builders of Lindbergh's *Spirit of St. Louis,* had modified his own plane before flying it non-stop from Long Beach, California, to New York. He submitted applications for permission to make a non-stop flight from the U.S. to Ireland, but his request was hung up in various offices. Irritated by the delay, Corrigan filed a flight plan which called for a return to Long Beach, but rather than heading west he pointed his tiny craft eastward across the water. Later he claimed that his unauthorized flight from

Floyd Bennett Field in Brooklyn to Ireland was caused by heavy cloud cover and low light conditions that obscured landmarks; he simply had made a "navigational error." More likely, it was his way of protesting against red tape in government.

Air travel was still hazardous, and a crash in remote Alaska made headlines in 1935. Legendary Wiley Post was a test pilot and air-mail pilot who had won international fame in 1931 when he, along with companion Harold Gatty, had flown around the earth in eight days, fifteen hours, and fifty-one minutes. Two years later, Post made virtually the same flight alone. His around-the-world solo flight was the most exciting aerial event of that year.

Post's high-wing monoplane for his historic journey around the world, the *Winnie Mae*, was very fragile and his navigation was done mainly by the "seat of his pants." He used a Michelin road map to guide him from Berlin to Moscow, for example, and from Moscow he headed for Novosibirsk. Lost and forced to land in a meadow, peasants surrounded his plane and with gestures were able to point him toward his destination.

Post was not the only hero of the skies in 1935. In that year, James Mattern had attempted an almost identical flight but crashed and was lost in Siberia for more than three months before being rescued. J. R. Weddell set a record of 305 miles per hour at the International Air Races in Chicago, and Frank Hawks established a new nonstop transcontinental record by flying from Los Angeles to New York in the fantastic time of 13 hours, 25 minutes and 14 seconds.[2]

Humorist Will Rogers of Oklahoma was a good friend of Wiley Post. As a cowboy on Oklahoma ranches, Rogers had developed skill as a rider and "rope twirler." In addition to an unusual gift for wry humor, he became an entertainer of kings and commoners. He went to Hollywood and starred in features and shorts during the cinema's silent era. In August 1935, Post and Rogers were together flying in Alaska when their craft went down near Point Barrow; they both died instantly.

Two writers giving a factual narrative of the Post/Rogers flight allege that the crash was Post's responsibility. Bryan and Frances Sterling argue that the aircraft Post was flying was uninspected and nose-heavy from the very start; the addition of pontoons made it even more so. Also, according to these two authors, Post had little experience in piloting a plane with pontoons and had ignored advice from Alaskan hands not to fly in the heavy fog around Point Barrow.[3]

Air travel included more than just airplanes. World War I had seen both England and Germany building rigid airships, i.e. large latticework structures filled with gas. Such dirigibles had propellers jutting outside the structure and were driven by engines within it. Mounted as an undercarriage of the airship, there were flight controls and room for whatever passengers designers meant to accommodate.

In 1919, a British dirigible named simply the *R34* crossed the Atlantic. Flying from England to America, this airship made the crossing and returned to its home base in a flight of 75 hours. For nearly two decades following the First World War, it was Germany, however, that took the lead in building airships. The *Graf Zeppelin I*, built there in 1926-1927, made a spectacular flight of 20,000 miles around the world in 1929. Following *Graf Zeppelin I* came an even larger dirigible christened the *Hindenburg*.

The first week of May 1937, amidst great publicity, the *Hindenburg* had come to America. On the final day of its life, the graceful airship had flown around New England's coast before permitting its 97 awed and impressed passengers to gaze at the skyscrapers of New York City. Violent storms were in the area as the craft wafted its way toward a mooring mast at the Naval Air Station at Lakehurst, New Jersey. On the ground there an excited crowd of more than 250 persons had gathered to watch the landing. Threatening clouds were everywhere, but there seemed to be no lightning around the naval base itself.

Captain Max Pruss, piloting the *Hindenburg*, decided it was safe to land. Slowly, the mammoth hydrogen-filled balloon began its descent. When it was down to about 300 feet, a blue ring suddenly appeared around the tail end of the monster. The ring expanded, moved forward quickly, and within seconds the silver airship was ablaze. With skeletal rib structures showing through the blaze, the ship fell, and its terrified passengers had only seconds to get out. A few passengers—some already on fire—jumped out windows of the undercarriage when the airship was down to fifty or forty feet. Others tried to ride it to the ground, and while horrified spectators watched, the ship crashed to the earth. The entire disaster had taken less than thirty-five seconds. Thirty-six persons died in the tragedy, including several members of the ground crew who gave their lives as they endeavored to save the *Hindenburg's* stricken occupants.

Pilot Max Pruss was badly burned but survived. Captain Emil Lehmann, commander of the flight, was also horribly burned. He died from his injuries but lived long enough to assert that he believed the disaster could only have been caused by sabotage. There were suspicions, never proved, and most historians came to believe that a spark from surrounding storms had ignited the dirigible's highly flammable hydrogen. One fact was indisputable; weather had been a perfect scenario, playing a key role in the disaster. After the *Hindenburg* tragedy, Germany dismantled its *Graf Zeppelin I* and its successor the *Graf Zeppelin II*. Remnants of both creations were sold for scrap.

CHAPTER 7:
ENTERTAINMENT & RECREATION

RADIO

Throughout most of America, evenings during Depression years were stay-at-home ones spent over Ouja boards, Monopoly games, jigsaw puzzles or solitaire—a routine broken by a weekly band concert in the town square during summer months, sometimes a quilting bee for the women in winter, or an annual family reunion in spring, summer, or fall, with grandparents and spread-out relations of uncles, aunts, and cousins attending.

For five evenings a week, families fortunate enough to have radios would tune in to hear fabled broadcasters give a fifteen-minute review of the news. Among the leading figures were H. V. Kaltenborn, Gabriel Heater, and Lowell Thomas. Thomas brought a sense of adventure into the living room.

Born in 1892 in Woodington, Ohio, Thomas had grown up in Cripple Creek, Colorado. He made his first sojourn to European battlefields during World War I, and after that debacle had ended and before entering radio, he traveled the world writing and lecturing. Thomas began daily broadcasts on NBC in 1930 and pioneered radio journalism with a career that spanned fifty years. When people heard his standard opening—"Good evening, everybody"—and his closing—"So long until tomorrow"—listeners knew they were hearing a solid, objective voice of authority.

Five nights a week—Mondays through Fridays—radio listeners in living rooms put aside their own troubles to hear those of Amos n' Andy. The two fictitious characters were created by Freeman F. Gosden and Charles J. Correll, white men and former producers of home talent revues. The two had begun careers as a comic harmony team called Sam n' Henry on Chicago radio in 1925. Three years later radio station WMAQ in that city introduced Amos Jones and Andy Brown as hired hands on a farm outside Atlanta, looking ahead to their planned move to Chicago. Amos was plagued by self-doubts, but the swaggering Andy was quick with answers to everything.

In the North, the two had a friend who persuaded them to start the Fresh Air Taxicab Company. They also met a successful middle-class businessman who had an attractive daughter named Ruby, and she eventually became Amos's fiancée. Another character adding humor to the show was George "Kingfish" Stevens—potentate of a local fraternity and a smooth hustler who insinuated himself into the affairs of the two central characters.

Within a few months, Amos n' Andy had attracted a national following. In the series, Amos was presented as a sympathetic figure with practical intelligence and gritty determination. Andy, by contrast, was a windy braggart, obsessed with the trappings of success. The Kingfish was a shrewd, resourceful man who lived by his wits rather than applying his time and talent to any real business.

Throughout the Depression Era, money-making schemes of the Kingfish moved in and out of the various plots. Amos represented traditional economic values, believing that wealth had to be earned; the Kingfish embodied Wall Street's lure of easy money; and Andy stood in the middle, an investor torn between prudence and greed. Amos n' Andy gave the public an allegory of what had happened to America in the 1920s.

Witty George Bernard Shaw once remarked, "There are three things I will never forget about America—Niagara Falls, the Rocky Mountains, and Amos n' Andy." Nevertheless, by the end of the 1930s decade, the Amos n' Andy series was drawing criticism from some African-Americans for its dialect and lower-class characterizations. Yet the shows had a sizeable audience of black supporters. Throughout Amos n' Andy's fantastic run, African-American opinion remained divided on its interpretation of the complex, often contradictory racial images portrayed.[1]

MOVIES

For twenty years following World War I, numerous movies put out by Hollywood gave the public strong anti-war themes. One of the most remarkable early films was *All Quiet on the Western Front*, based on a novel first written in German (*Im Westen nichts Neues*) in 1929 by Erich Maria Remarque, a veteran of the First World War. The film showed the horrors of trench warfare as well as the deep attachment to German civilian life felt by men returning from the front. Released in 1930, *All Quiet on the Western Front* proved to be an Oscar winner.

On a lighter note, a comedy written by Robert E. Sherwood in 1936 presented equally strong pacifist and ardent antifascist themes. Sherwood's *Idiots Delight* presented scenes set in an area ceded to Italy after WW I National borders had been closed, and the drama gave viewers and readers a plot in which guests sitting at a cocktail bar were certain the next war was about to begin. The characters could only wonder who would be the belligerents; the map of Europe allowed such a wide choice. *Idiot's Delight* won a Pulitzer Prize and years later (1983) was turned into an unsuccessful musical called *Dance a Little Closer*.

Throughout the Depression years small theaters—Rialto, Strand, Orpheum, Collegian, or Bijou—drew millions of viewers each week. Movies were cheap; in bigger cities only 45 or 50 cents for adults, and 10 cents for youngsters below twelve. In addition to the films presented, theaters offered other inducements—drawings in which lucky winners captured prizes like free passes, groceries, dishes, kitchen utensils, household furniture, or actual cash during the popular "Bank Nites."

In darkened theaters one could smooth the roughness that came from daily living, for inside the theater there was anonymity—anonymity for teenagers holding hands in the back rows or for older viewers who had come to escape work or other duties. Comedies, improbable westerns, adventure sagas, and happy tales of love-conquers-all permitted a person to live out his or her wildest fancy.

The format seldom varied. First would be a cartoon featuring Felix the Cat, later Mickey Mouse or another Walt Disney character, then Fox or Movietone News, followed with blaring announcements of forthcoming attractions. Then, with suitable ballyhoo, the feature attraction would be introduced.

Comedies were popular, and in 1934 a romantic one entitled *It Happened One Night* starring Clark Gable and Claudette Colbert titillated movie goers everywhere. In addition to light stories of that sort, there were farces with the antics of the Marx brothers—Chico, Harpo, Groucho, Gummo, and Zeppo.

In 1937, Walt Disney released *Snow White and the Seven Dwarfs*—a film based on a fairy tale by the same name written by The Brothers Grimm. *Snow White* was the first full-length animated movie and ushered in another dimension to the industry.

It was not until near the end of the decade, however, that the real blockbuster movie came out, and that was *Gone with the Wind*. A Georgia housewife, Margaret Mitchell, had written the book, first published in 1936. The story set in the American South in and around the time of the Civil War tells of the slaughtering in that conflict and its social and economic aftermaths. The narrative has all the elements of pure drama: history (noticeably from a Southern viewpoint), romance, and adventure. As stars, directors chose Clark Gable, Olivia de Havilland, and Leslie Howard, along with a beautiful young actress from Britain, Vivien Leigh, who played the tempestuous Scarlett O'Hara.

Two weeks before the close of the thirties, the movie—three years in the making—premiered in Atlanta, Georgia, where citizens went all out to promote it. Women put on hoop skirts and pantalets; men donned light trousers and sprouted side-burns, goatees, handle-bar or Rhett Butler mustaches. Vivien Leigh, aka Scarlett O'Hara, showed up, as did her co-star Clark Gable with his glamorous wife, Carole Lombard. At a costume ball the night before the public showing, one young girl, enamored by the Gable persona, gasped, "Lord, I can't stand this any longer," and fainted dead away!

At tiny Christian College in Columbia, Missouri, Josephine Dillon, the school's drama coach, watched her former spouse Clark Gable and said, "The part calls for a big, dashing, handsome man who can really act. I saw my ex-husband, and he was magnificent. He hasn't forgotten a thing I taught him."

The film *Gone with the Wind* received ten Academy Awards and sold more tickets than any other movie in history. The movie would be shown in theaters for the next seventy years, would be aired on countless reruns when television came into existence, and would take its place as one of the most enduring symbols of Hollywood in its golden age.

MUSIC

If the twenties featured bathtub gin, raccoon coats, bobbed hair, and flappers, the 1930s was an era of music. Radio brought it into thousands of American homes. A listener sitting in his living room could hear melodies ranging from grand opera to bluegrass. Radio broadcast it all and especially helped engineer the expansion of performances by symphony orchestras. Arturo Toscanini was made conductor of the New York Philharmonic and later became organizer as well as conductor of the National Broadcasting Company's Symphony Orchestra.

Often, too, music was presented in public concerts. Fiorello LaGuardia, Mayor of New York City, arranged to bring "long-haired" music to the man on the street." Under the mayor's auspices, top-flight Metropolitan stars such as Lauritz Melchior, Elisabeth Rethberg, and Friedrich Schorr were engaged to sing with the Works Progress Administration's (WPA) New York City Symphony. Moreover, *Hizzoner* sponsored a series of Wagnerian concerts at Rockefeller's Center Theatre, where seats were sold for bargain basement prices of twenty-five cents to one dollar.

The Jazz Age of Scott Fitzgerald and Sophie Tucker had ended by 1930, only to be replaced by big-named bands, made popular by Hollywood and radio. Big bands were in their heyday—the venerable Paul Whiteman, Glenn Miller, Woody Herman, Duke Ellington, Tommy and Jimmy Dorsey, Guy Lombardo, Harry James, Les Brown, and Louie Armstrong, to name a few.

One band leader, Orrin Tucker, resurrected a tune called *"Oh, Johnny, Oh,"* and gave it to his vocalist "Wee Bonny Baker." Her revival of the old melody rapidly climbed to a top spot on radio's *Your Hit Parade*, sponsored by Lucky Strike cigarettes, and sold more than 350,000 records even before hitting the jukeboxes.

Nickel jukeboxes were everywhere—restaurants, cafes, tea rooms, taverns, variety stores, gasoline stations, and barber shops. A patron could hear ten records for fifty cents, and at least one entrepreneur offered three minutes of silence for a tenth of that amount.

SPORTS

The so-called Press-Radio War in America—competition which started in the twenties—had begun easing in the thirties and was replaced by rivalries among emerging radio networks. Networks vied to cover special events, such as interviews, trials, accidents, and sporting news.

The first big sporting events in which broadcasting "rights" were sold were heavyweight boxing matches. The National Broadcasting Company was founded in 1926 and in that year, it was estimated the greatest radio audience to date had gathered at loud speakers to hear ringside accounts of the Dempsey-Tunney fight. In 1927, the Columbia Broadcasting System was organized and competition between it and NBC followed.

Network rivalries escalated until the mid 1930s; by this time most of the major sports events had been "sewed up." American Broadcasting Company had championship fights, NBC the Rose Bowl, Mutual Broadcasting System the World Series in baseball, and CBS the Kentucky Derby.

In retrospect, some of the antics used by competing network crews seem far-fetched. Paul W. White, long-time Director of News for CBS, tells about rivalries between his network and the National Broadcasting Company when the latter had an "exclusive" arrangement with the Amateur Athletic Union to cover the annual contest sponsored by the Amateur Athletic Union and held in Milwaukee, Wisconsin.

The arrangement kept Ted Husing, veteran CBS sports announcer, from getting his microphone into the stadium, but he did manage to get permission from a Lutheran pastor to set up his gear on the roof of a church-owned schoolhouse overlooking the track event. Learning of Husing's intentions, an NBC executive complained to Milwaukee city officials that Husing was erecting a platform "without securing a building permit." Unsuccessful with that protest, NBC next considered blocking Husing's view by hanging up hundreds of yards of cheesecloth but were unable to find such a vast amount of cheesecloth in the city.

Perhaps in whimsy, Paul White listed other ideas weighed by his NBC rivals:

1. Hiring a brigade of small boys to shine sun reflections into Husing's eyes by means of small hand-held mirrors.

2. Persuading track meet officials to confuse Husing by hanging wrong numbers on the athletes.

3. Hiring an airplane to fly over the schoolhouse roof and confuse the announcer by dropping things on him. It was hoped, too, that the roar of the motor could drown out Husing's voice.

4. Hiring a South American blow-gun artist to pick off Husing with a poison dart.

5. Arranging with a firm of building wreckers to tear the building down right from under Husing.

All of these plans had to be abandoned because it was the third of July and people got so independent thinking about Independence Day that you couldn't get anybody to do any work, much less dirty work.[2]

In the decade of the 1920s, sports enthusiasts followed exploits of Jack Dempsey, Babe Ruth, Bobby Jones, Helen Wills, Gertrude Ederle, Babe Didrikson, Red Grange, and the Four Horsemen of Notre Dame.

Often considered the greatest female athlete of the twentieth century, nee Mildred Ella Didrikson was more familiarly known as Babe. Also called the Texas Tornado, the Amazing Amazon, or the Terrific Tomboy, Didrikson was a track-and-field champion, All-American basketball star, record-setting golfer, and all-around force in everything from baseball to bowling. Asked once if there were anything she didn't play, she responded, "Yeah! Dolls."

Didrikson's stellar career was marked by over two decades of honors: gold medal (1932 Olympics, 80 meter hurdles); gold medal (1932 Olympics, javelin); silver medal (1932 Olympics, high jump); Champion (1947 British Open golf tournament); elected to LPGA Hall of Fame 1951; Associated Press Female Athlete of the Year, 1932, 1945-47, 1950, and 1954.

The Associate Press summarized Didrikson's remarkable career by stating,

"The pert, wiry Texan never found a game she couldn't play better than everyone else."

Blacks, then relegated to rundown neighborhoods and flophouses and considered inferior by many white citizens, established world records in sports. In boxing rings, Jack Johnson was the first black world champion, and in years just prior to World War II, the name of Jesse Owns dominated sport pages.

James Cleveland Owens, grandson of a slave and son of a sharecropper, was born in Alabama, and when he was nine years old moved with his parents to Ohio. He tried to tell a Cleveland teacher his name was *J. C. Owens*, but she did not understand his southern accent, and his name of *Jesse* was created.

Owens first came to national attention in 1933 when, as a high school student, he equaled the world record of 9.4 seconds in the 100-yard dash and leaped 24 feet, 9½ inches at the National High School Championship in Chicago. He attended Ohio State University, and during his student years there won a record of eight individual NCAA championships, four each in 1935 and 1936. While enjoying unparalleled athletic successes, Owens had to live off campus, and during travels with the team could either order "carry outs" or eat at "black only" restaurants. In 1936, Owens arrived in Berlin, Germany, to compete for the U.S. in the summer Olympics. Adolph Hitler and other high Nazi officials were using the games to promote ideas of Aryan superiority, depicting non-Aryans, and Afro-Americans in particular, as inferior races. Owens surprised many by winning a stunning total of four gold medals. On the fourth day, when Owens won his fourth medal, Hitler left the stadium without presenting the awards. On reports that Hitler had deliberately avoided acknowledging his victories and had refused to shake his hand, Owens had this to say:

"When I passed the Chancellor he waved his hand at me, and I waved back at him. I think the writers showed bad taste in criticizing the man of the hour in Germany. . . . Hitler didn't snub me—it was FDR who snubbed me. The President didn't even send me a telegram."[3]

Throughout the 1930s, radio listeners, newspaper readers, movie-goers, and sports fans everywhere followed professional boxing and especially the career of Joe Louis. Louis, considered by many fistic experts to have been the greatest Heavyweight Boxing Champion in the sport's history, was the seventh child of an Alabama sharecropper. In 1934 as an amateur, he won three of the nation's most prestigious boxing tournaments: the Michigan Golden Gloves, the National AAU, and the Chicago Golden Gloves Tournament of Champions. Late in that year, he turned professional and knocked out his first opponent in the bout's opening round. He won his next ten fights—all by knockouts.

In 1935, Louis fought thirteen bouts, winning them all, including a knockout of a former world champion, the 6'6", 235 pound Primo Canera. In another match that year, he knocked out another former heavyweight world champion, the iron-chinned Max Baer, who had never been knocked out or even downed before.

In his next fight, Louis was matched against former world champion, Germany's Max Schmeling. The German had studied Louis's style intently, and in the twelfth round at Yankee Stadium was able to knock Louis out, handing the American his first professional loss.

Despite that loss to Schmeling, Louis's managers were able to arrange a title shot for him against the reigning world champion, James Braddock. Louis won his match against Braddock by a knockout in the eighth round. Now his promoters could claim he was the world's champion.

Schmeling and the Nazi government disagreed, and even after Louis won a match against the highly-ranked Jack Sharkey, Nazis insisted that neither fight in America reversed the win Schmeling had accomplished over Louis.

Negotiations for a rematch between Louis and Schmeling got underway. Following his defeat of Louis in 1935, Schmeling had become a hero in Germany; Nazis touted his defeat of an African-American as proof of "Aryan superiority." The second fight between Louis and Schmeling is often hyped as the most famous boxing match of all time; certainly it was one of the major sports events of the twentieth century.

When Schmeling arrived in New York City for the match, he was accompanied by Nazi party officials who issued statements to the effect that a black man could not defeat Schmeling, and that when their champion won, his prize money would be used to build tanks and armaments for the Fatherland.

Ironically, while most Americans associated Schmeling with the Nazi party, he never joined it, and indeed once refused to accept an award from Adolph Hitler. His resistance to the Nazi party won respect in the post-war period, and Schmeling became a life-long friend of his rival, Joe Louis.

On the night of June 22, 1938, Louis and Schmeling met in a boxing ring for the second time. The match was held in Yankee Stadium before a crowd of 70,043 and was broadcast by radio to millions throughout the world, with ringside announcers reporting in English, German, Spanish, and Portuguese. Schmeling had weighed in at 193 pounds, Louis at 198.5 pounds.

The bout lasted two minutes and four seconds. Louis battered Schmeling with a series of swift attacks, forcing Schmeling against the ropes and pummeling him with paralyzing body blows. Schmeling was knocked down three times and only managed to throw three punches in the entire bout. On the third knockdown, Schmeling's trainer threw in the towel, and referee Arthur Donovan stopped the fight.

In all, Louis made 25 defenses of his heavyweight title from 1937 to 1949. He was a world champion for 11 years and 10 months, setting a record in number of defenses and longevity as world champion, nonstop; most remarkably, he knocked out 23 opponents in 27 fights.

Louis served in the U.S. Army from 1942 to 1945 and spent that period traveling around Europe visiting with troops and giving boxing exhibitions. Years after his retirement, and only hours after his last public appearance, on April 12, 1981, the sixty-six-year-old Joe Louis died of a heart attack.

U.S. President Ronald Reagan waived eligibility rules for burial at Arlington National Cemetery, and Louis was buried there with full military honors. His life and achievements prompted one sportswriter to offer an epitaph: "Joe Louis is a credit to his race—the human race."[4]

LITERATURE & FINE ARTS

Without jobs and incomes, many Americans could not afford to attend stage plays or movies, so they turned to libraries and books. Publisher Henry Luce had started the popular news magazine *Time* in 1923; thirteen years later he took another, almost immediately successful plunge, with *Life*, a pictorial magazine of current events.

Libraries were magnets for citizens in towns fortunate enough to have them, and smaller, lower-priced paperback editions named *Pocketbooks* first appeared in the U. S. as the decade closed. Paperback publications were immediately popular and spread like wildfire, particularly among persons traveling or away from home.

A popular writer of the period was Sinclair Lewis. His *Main Street* (1920), a satire on small town life in the American Middle West, was read in the U.S. and abroad. His next novel, *Babbitt* (1922) described the typical American businessman and was equally acclaimed. In *Arrowsmith* (1925), Lewis wrote about a medical doctor and idealist, who fell in love and married a trusting, faithful nurse. Serving together in the Caribbean area, Dr. Arrowsmith is tempted by another woman; he never really cheats on his wife but is sorely tempted. Thus in presenting his fiction, writer Lewis makes lust in the heart equal and as serious a sin as actual adultery.

Other books that helped Lewis win plaudits were *Elmer Gantry* (1927) and *Dodsworth* (1929). Lewis's broad-stroke satirical novels presenting their devastating pictures of the middle class won him a Pulitzer Prize, which he declined, but in 1930 he accepted the Nobel Prize in Literature, becoming the first American writer to win it.

Although in 1930 Sinclair Lewis won the Nobel Prize for Literature, many American readers and critics believed the award should have gone to one of his contemporaries, Theodore Dreiser. Dreiser's first historic novel had come with the publication of *Sister Carrie*, a story of a young girl who runs off with a married man. The novel was controversial and banned in several cities because of its seamy descriptions of urban life. *Sister Carrie*, nevertheless, established Dreiser's reputation as a first-rate novelist, and he continued to write in different genres—criticisms, reviews, and fiction. In the last-named category he achieved his most notable success.

In 1925, Dreiser finished writing *An American Tragedy*, a story of an aspiring young man who came to the city and got involved with a girl from an economic background similar to his own. In his climb toward financial and social success, the boy falls in love with the daughter of his rich employer. However, by this time his first love has become pregnant and insists on their marriage. The distraught boy contrives to drown her, but soon after that tragic event he is arrested and charged with her murder. In jail and facing death because appeals for clemency have been denied, the novel ends with the boy being led into the execution chambers.

An American Tragedy became Dreiser's best seller and the masterpiece for which he is mainly remembered. By the opening of the 1930s, Dreiser was recognized as a warrior battling for literary freedoms everywhere. In the latter years of that decade, readers knew him almost as much through his public statements as through his creative writings. Dreiser's political views were not always popular, but they were not unusual among intellectuals prior to the bombing of Pearl Harbor.

Dreiser traveled to Russia and came back to America praising aspects of the revolution which he said was striving to better the lives of its citizens. Although he came to despise the totalitarianism of the Soviet Government, he remained adamantly opposed to British and other moneyed interests.

In July, 1945, five months before his death, Dreiser made his last dramatic gesture by joining the Communist Party. In a final public statement, he tried to sum up reasons for that action: "Belief in the greatness and dignity of Man has been the guiding principle of my life and work. The logic of my life and work leads me, therefore, to apply for membership in the Communist Party." His strength clearly ebbing, Theodore Dreiser died of heart failure on December 28, 1945.

Another writer of the period was Pearl Buck, nee Pearl Comfort Sydenstricker, born in Hillsboro, West Virginia, in 1892. She was the fourth of seven children born to missionary parents who spent most of their adult lives in China. Pearl was taken there with them when they ended a brief furlough in the U.S., and she would spend more than forty years of her own life in that land.

The young Pearl Sydenstricker was guided by a Chinese tutor and learned to speak both English and Chinese in early childhood. In 1910, her parents returned to America for another furlough, and Pearl was enrolled at Randolph-Macon Women's College in Lynchburg, Virginia, graduating from there four years later. She went back to China almost immediately and, in 1915, married an agricultural economist named John Lossing Buck. It was a rocky marriage, but one which lasted seventeen years, during which Pearl Buck amassed materials she would find useful in her masterful story *The Good Earth*.

For thirteen years, 1920 until 1933, Pearl and her husband John Lossing made their home in Nanking, where both had teaching positions at the university. In 1927, violence broke out in what became known as the "Nanking Incident," and in confrontations between Nationalist and Communist forces, assorted warlords and several westerners were killed. Although conditions in Nanking remained dangerously unsettled, Pearl Buck remained there for another six years.

Buck had begun writing, and her first book was published by America's John Day Company in 1930. Pearl and her husband Lossing agreed to end their unstable marriage, and in 1935 she married Richard Walsh, an executive at the John Day Company. With his encouragement, the company in 1931 published *The Good Earth*, Buck's second novel. The book became an immediate best-seller, winning the Pulitzer Prize, the Howells Medal, and becoming a hit movie put out by MGM in 1937. The next year—a decade after her first book had been published—Pearl Buck won the Nobel Prize in literature, the first American woman to do so.

Largely due to conditions in China and concern for a daughter retarded enough to be institutionalized, Pearl Buck moved back to the U.S., establishing her home in Pennsylvania. From the day of her return to America, she was very active in civil and women's rights, publishing essays in *Crisis*, the journal of the NAACP, *Opportunity*—the magazine of the Urban League—and was a trustee of Howard University. In 1942, Pearl Buck and her husband Richard Walsh founded the East and West Association, a group dedicated to establishing cultural exchange and understanding between the continents.

In 1973, just two months before her eighty-first birthday, the prolific and talented Pearl Buck died. She is buried at Green Hills Farm in Bucks County, Pa., now a historic site visited by more than fifteen thousand people each year.[5]

The harsh life of the thirties in the U.S. inspired writers like Erskine Caldwell, Studs Terkel, and John Steinbeck. Perhaps Steinbeck's most lasting contribution was *Grapes of Wrath*, a story of Oklahoma families displaced by dust or drought and attempting to move into paradisiacal California. The epic was later made into a very successful movie.

Other popular and award winning movies of the Depression included *Dr. Jeckyl and Mr. Hyde* (1931), *The Champ* (1931), *The Private Life of Henry VIII* (1932), *It Happened One Night* (1934), *Mutiny on the Bounty* (1935), *The Story of Louis Pasteur* (1936), *Life of Emile Zola* (1937), *You Can't Take It With You* (1938), the sensational *Gone With The Wind* (1939), and *Rebecca* (1940). Thornton Wilder's lachrymose *Our Town* was first produced on Broadway in 1938, and would become a perennial favorite among high school and college groups for the next ten generations.[6]

RANDOM NEWS & EVENTS

With the nation in deep depression and with hopes of bolstering the economy the Century of Progress Exposition (Chicago World's Fair) opened in March, 1933. It closed in the following November but reopened in May, 1934. It closed again when that October rolled around, and sponsors declared the enterprise a huge success, drawing a total attendance of more than 8,626,546 persons.

A featured attraction at the Chicago Exposition was Sally Rand (nee Harriet Helen Gould Beck), an American icon. A dancer at an early age, she ran away with a carnival as a teenager. After her experience with the carnival and two failed marriages, she danced with a ballet company, joined Ringling Brothers Circus, and appeared on stage with such luminaries as Eddie Cantor, Walter Winchell, and George Jessel. Her dancing and stage episodes led her to Hollywood, where she caught the attention of Cecil deMille, who gave her the name *Sally Rand*. Sally had bit parts in several silent films, but when "talkies" began to develop, a noticeable lisp foreclosed possibilities of her becoming a film star.

Rand's greatest reputation was gained from her appearances at Chicago's "Century of Progress" World's Fair in 1933. Most accounts report that Rand danced "in the nude" there, but in actuality she wore a tight-fitting body stocking while seductively maneuvering two seven-foot ostrich fans to titillate viewers.[7]

An event that aroused public interest in America happened near the village of Callendar in the province of Ontario, Canada, on May 24, 1934. There, with Dr. Allan Roy Dafoe and two midwives assisting, a mother gave birth to five identical little girls—the first quintuplets in recorded history to survive. Few in the rural community expected the Dionne infants to live, but they did.

The poverty-stricken parents kept the babies in their home for more than a year while government officials came to value the massive public interest in the rarity. In 1935, care for the babies was assumed by the government in Ontario, and the little girls were made wards of the provincial crown until they were 18. Meanwhile, across from the place where the babies had been born, entrepreneurs built the Dafoe Hospital and Nursery with the sole purpose of caring for the five infants. Souvenirs and quintuplet merchandise were sold in a theme-like park, and included in it was a gallery where thousands of visitors could watch through meshed screens as the young tots played twice a day.

For several years, *Quintland* surpassed even Niagara Falls as a tourist attraction. As they grew into maidenhood, the five Dionne girls asked that they be called sisters rather than quintuplets, but the world continued to think of the Dionne Quintuplets as one of nature's most unusual anomalies.

Half-way through the thirties, a romantic interlude titillated most of the civilized world. Wallis Warfield Simpson was a twice-married American socialite when at a house party she met Edward, Prince of Wales.

At 35, Wally Simpson was slightly beyond the first flush of youth and beauty, but she was seductive. Prince Edward, at the time the world's most eligible bachelor, was captivated. By January 1936, the Prince's infatuation for Wally Simpson had grown into an obsession. In the meantime though, he had ascended to the throne and become His Royal Highness Edward VIII.

The king's intention to marry a twice-divorced American woman with two living ex-husbands and a reputation as being an opportunist set off a constitutional crisis in the United Kingdom. Edward would not yield, however, and in December 1936 took to the air to announce to the world it was impossible for him to carry out his duties as king "without the woman I love." Edward abdicated his throne, and his brother, George VI, ascended to it, promptly giving the former king a title as Duke of Windsor.

Six months later, Edward and Wally Simpson married, and became the Duke and Duchess of Windsor—the latter without being recognized as "Her Royal Highness." The Duchess once explained, "You can't abdicate and eat it!"

Before, during, and after World War II, the Duke and his wife were suspected of being German sympathizers. The American Federal Bureau of Investigation was told that during the Nazi invasion of France in 1940 the duchess was said to have passed information to Joachim von Ribbentrop, the Nazis' foreign minister. Indeed, newspapers reported and showed pictures of the Duke and Duchess visiting Hitler at his mountain retreat at Berchtesgaden.

In the 1950s and 1960s, Edward and his wife traveled as society celebrities between Europe and the United States, living lives of leisure. After the Duke's death in 1972, his widow lived in seclusion and was rarely seen in public. The private life of Wallis Warfield Simpson, Duchess of Windsor, has been a source of much speculation, and she remains a controversial figure in British history.

On October 25, 1929—the birthday of the Great Depression—several persons who later would win occupancy of the nation's highest office were youths or not yet born.

Harry S Truman, who insisted there should be no period after the S in his middle name, was the Presiding Judge of the Jackson County Court in Missouri*. Dwight D. Eisenhower, a major in the U.S. Army, had been released from duties with the American Battle Monuments Commission and was in the process of being re-assigned as an assistant to the secretary of war in Washington, D.C.

Twelve-year-old John F. Kennedy, on his father's sumptuous estate near Hyannis Port, Massachusetts, was enjoying cultural, social, and economic advantages undreamt of by most American youths.

Lyndon Baines Johnson had obtained a teacher's certificate after two years of college, and, hard-pressed for money, had found a job teaching the fifth through seventh grades at Cotulla, an impoverished rural settlement halfway between San Antonio and Laredo, Texas, "a little, dried-up dying place," southwest of San Antonio and sixty miles north of the Mexican border.[9]

In 1929, Richard Milhous Nixon was a senior at Whittier High School in California, and Gerald R. Ford, nee Leslie R. King, Jr., who would become Vice President and move into the Oval Office upon Nixon's resignation, was in his final year at a Michigan high school. James Earl Carter, Jr., who wanted to be called Jimmy, celebrated his fifth birthday in Archery, a tiny rural community west of Plains, Georgia.

Ronald Wilson "Dutch" Reagan, in 1929, was an energetic high school junior in Dixon, Illinois, already serving as a lifeguard during summers at nearby Lowell Park, a three-hundred-acre forested area that fronted on the Rock River. In his autobiography, Reagan would insist that during those life-guarding years he saved seventy-seven people—his critics added: "whether they needed it or not."[10]

George Herbert Walker Bush, destined to become the nation's 41st president, was five years old and toddling around his parents' home in Milton, Massachusetts. Bill (William Jefferson) Clinton would not be born until a year after WW II had ended, nor would be George Walker Bush, eldest son of George H. W. Bush. The 44th President of the United States, Barack Obama, did not enter this world until August, 1961.

---

* The title "Judge" was honorary. Actually, Truman's position was more akin to what today would be known as a county commissioner.

CHAPTER 8: CRIME AND CRIMINALS

Crimes in America started with its founding and have flourished ever since, especially during hard times or military conflicts. Whether it be efforts to apprehend sea-going smugglers, find moonshiners in the hills, capture bootleggers, or enforce Prohibition laws, the battle against crime, random or organized, is a never-ending struggle.

World War I set off a crusading spirit in America. The country had gone to war under the slogan of making "the world safe for democracy," and by 1920, President Woodrow Wilson, although still in the White House, was ill and a lame-duck executive.

The U.S. Congress, in the last month of 1917, had passed the Eighteenth Amendment to the Constitution making the manufacturing, sale, or transportation of intoxicating liquors illegal. The Amendment was not ratified until January, two years later, but *Prohibition* was a law on the books. Almost immediately, people began to flout it. Men and women who otherwise considered themselves law-abiding citizens patronized bootleggers, carried pocket flasks, and at home concocted a peculiar brew or bathtub gin. The occupation of bootlegging reached gigantic proportions with the federal government trying in vain to stop it. Canadian and Mexican borders leaked like sieves as illicit traders smuggled in their liquors. Every major city in the United States became studded with "speakeasies," replacing the old-time saloons. In defiant states like Rhode Island, which refused either to ratify Amendment XVIII or help enforce it, one could buy a bottle of British gin right off the shelves of a grocery store for ten dollars.[1]

Nefarious characters in the eastern sections of the nation garnered gangs which perpetrated crimes of every variety—robberies, extortion, prostitution, drugs, illegal gambling, and murder. New York City and its environs were havens for racketeers like Frank Costello, Vito Genovese, Frank Abbandano, Louis Buchalter, and the kingpin of them all—Salvatore "Lucky" Luciano, a man who legally changed his name from *Luciana* to *Luciano* because as he said, "It was easier for cops to pronounce."

Jack "Legs" Diamond was an infamous Irish-American gangster in New York

City during the Prohibition Era. A flamboyant womanizer, his nickname "Legs" came from his nimbleness on the dance floor. Legs gained his most notoriety from overseeing bootleg alcohol sales in downtown Manhattan.

Another New York gangster, Joey Noe, set up the Hub Social Club, a hole-in-the-wall speakeasy. Noe hired Arthur "Dutch" Schultz to work in it, and soon Schultz became a partner, riding shotgun on trucks the two men had bought to deliver beer to the several branches of the original Hub Social Club. The Noe/Schultz enterprise prospered enough to attempt a move into Manhattan's Upper West Side, neighborhoods controlled by henchmen of Legs Diamond, and a full-scale war broke out between the two gangs.

Muscle men of the Schultz coterie kidnapped a rival underling, Joe Rock, from Diamond's crew, brutalized and beat him before hanging him by his thumbs on a meat hook. Then they allegedly wrapped a gauze bandage smeared with discharge from a gonorrhea infection over his eyes. As expected, shortly afterwards the victim went blind, but the message from the Noe/Schultz gang had been clear.

Conflicts, brutalities, and deaths occurred for more than seven years as members from the two rival forces fought one another. Diamond was rubbed out when, in the middle of December, 1931, at a late night party in Albany, New York, he was shot three times in the back of the head.

In the subsequent four years, the career of Dutch Schultz grew even more convoluted. Unable to find sufficient evidence to charge Schultz with murders, U.S. Attorney Thomas E. Dewey opted to bring him to court for evasion of federal income tax payments. To help with defense strategy and court expenses, Schultz went to the kingpin, Lucky Luciano. With Luciano presiding over other members of the so-called Mafia Commission, Schultz proposed a bizarre scheme for assassinating his nemesis, Thomas Dewey. Luciano called the plan "insane," and others on the Commission agreed with him, believing the murder of such a public figure as Dewey would bring the full weight of authorities down on all of them.

Schultz felt he had been betrayed by Luciano, and his animosity smoldered. It was he, however, who paid the price. On October 23, 1935, Schultz, along with two bodyguards and his accountant, were gunned down at the Palace Chophouse in Newark, New Jersey. When police arrived at the scene, they gave Schultz brandy, hoping to keep him alive long enough for the ride to the hospital. There emergency surgery was performed, but the doctors were unaware that rusty bullets had been used in the belief that if they did not kill Schultz immediately a later infection would. Schultz died of peritonitis seventy-two hours after being shot.

Another incident in municipal gang wars, high or low depending upon one's view, was the 1929 Valentine Day's Massacre in Chicago. In the Windy City Al "Scarface" Capone ran a gang of hoodlums on the south side; George "Bugs" Moran a similar one on the north. Dion O'Banion, cheap thug and member of the north side gang, wore a string of rosary beads over his vest, right next to his shoulder holster. O'Banion was noted for giving $100 to defray funeral costs of rival gangsters, and it was said that for a few extra dollars he also would provide the corpse. His favorite weapon was the "Tommy" gun—a gangster's dream, for it fired 800 rounds of .45 caliber ammunition per minute and required only minimal skill to spray an automobile or an apartment.

Al Capone had gotten started by hijacking and selling bootleg liquor, and by the late 1920s his mob had made Chicago one of the most crime-ridden cities in the world. In four years, there had been 215 unsolved murders, widely attributed to warfare between Capone and Moran gangs. "You can get further with a kind word and a gun," Capone once had proclaimed, "than you can with a gun alone."

On February 14, 1929, Capone thugs, disguised as policemen, machine-gunned six of the Moran gang who were in a garage waiting to buy a truckload of liquor from hijackers. The six victims were lined up against the wall and drilled with "Chicago typewriters." No one was punished for the atrocity, although two years later, at the opening of the next decade, Capone was indicted by a federal grand jury for evasion of income tax payments and sentenced to an eleven-year prison term.

The bells of Repeal rang out in the last month of the year 1933; on the day that Utah became the 39th state to ratify the Twenty-first Amendment. The Eighteenth Amendment, the only one ever to be rolled back, banning liquor sales was notable in clarity and brevity: "The eighteenth article of amendment to the Constitution of the United States is hereby repealed." President Franklin Roosevelt reportedly mixed the nation's first legal martini in nearly fourteen years.

Prohibition had not achieved its goal of eliminating liquor consumption; moreover, enforcement of the law had proved to be expensive as well as impossible. Temperance leaders—many of whom happened to be women—had lost the battle; indeed, after Repeal many of them joined the opposition. Not among the renegades, though, was the doughty Carry Nation, a six-foot tall Kansas Amazon who lost one husband to alcohol and a second to her activism.

In the spring of 1900, Carry Nation loaded a wagon with brickbats, bottles, bits of scrap metal, and chunks of wood, before traveling twenty-five miles from her home to a town where she laid waste to three saloons, smashed windows, glassware, and artwork. Attempts to arrest her came to nothing at the time because Kansas was a "dry" state. Her efforts spread to other states, but in those "wet" ones she hectored, shouted, and railed rather than destroyed physical property.

In 1910, Carry Nation led her final crusade in Butte, Montana, where she was confronted by a woman saloon owner with determination equal to her own. Not long after this confrontation, Nation died of "nervous trouble" and was buried, largely forgotten, in a small cemetery in Missouri.[2]

During the thirties, kidnapping replaced the liquor racketeering of the preceding decade as the nation's prime crime. By far the most sensational kidnapping was seizure of nineteen-month-old Charles Lindbergh, Jr. Baltimore scribe H. L Mencken called it "the biggest story since the Resurrection."

A nurse had tucked the infant in bed at the regular time, but when she went to check on him two hours later, she discovered the tot was missing. She immediately informed Mrs. Anne Morrow Lindbergh. A handwritten letter, riddled with spelling errors and grammatical irregularities, was discovered on the nursery window sill, and outside a shoddy, homemade ladder had been placed, reaching from the ground to the second floor window.

Word of the kidnapping spread quickly, for the baby was heir of the most idolized man of the twenties. Persons ranging from Al Capone in prison and Herbert Hoover in the White House offered to help. The Bureau of Investigation, not yet called the FBI, was authorized to investigate the case, and the U.S. Customs Service, the Coast Guard, the Immigration Service, and the Washington, D.C. police were alerted and told their assistance might be required. Despite numerous false leads and complications, for an agonizingly long time no real progress was made toward finding the child or the culprits.

Following instructions contained in mysterious letters, a ransom of $100,000 was paid in gold certificates, which at the time were being withdrawn from circulation.[3] It was hoped that anyone passing large amounts of gold certificates would attract attention and thus aid in identifying the kidnapper or kidnappers.

Two and a half months later, a corpse identified as Charles Lindbergh, Jr., the missing baby, was found. The body, decomposed, its skull fractured, and with one leg and both hands missing, was discovered within four and a half miles from the Lindbergh home.

Two years after the infant's seizure, Bruno Richard Hauptmann, a German immigrant with a criminal record in his own homeland, was arrested after passing a $10 gold certificate from the ransom money. Police searches found more than $15,000 of the ransom money hidden away or under his garage in the Bronx.

Arrested for kidnapping and charged with murder of the child, there was a sensational, drawn-out trial before Hauptmann was convicted and sentenced to death by electrocution. Numerous appeals were rejected, although New Jersey Governor Harold G. Hoffman granted Hauptmann a temporary reprieve to permit the state's Board of Pardons to review the case. Not finding sufficient reasons to overturn the verdict, the execution was performed on April 3, 1936, four years after the kidnapping.

An important result of the Lindbergh kidnapping was passage of the 1932 Federal Kidnapping Act, popularly called the Lindbergh Law. This statute made it a federal offense to kidnap someone with the intent to seek a ransom or reward. The law would be modified in several ways not only to increase penalties but to make investigative work of government agents easier.

The Lindbergh Law failed to halt all kidnappings, however, and a rash of others followed. On February 1, 1933, Charles Boettcher of Denver was taken, held for nearly a month but then released at the beginning of March unharmed. In May 1933, Mary McElroy of Kansas City was kidnapped, released almost immediately, and her captor, Walter McGee, sentenced to life imprisonment. In July 1933, three men and a woman were convicted of kidnapping August Luer; the captors were ordered to serve life sentences.

In that month of July alone, John J. O'Connell, Jr., was taken from his home in Albany, N.Y., and that crime was followed by the kidnapping of Charles F. Urschel of Oklahoma City. Urschel was released after nine days of captivity, but his captors, George "Machine Gun" Kelly and five accomplices, were seized and sentenced to terms of life in prison.

A kidnapping with a sensational aftermath took place in San Jose, California, when on November 9, 1933, Brook L. Hart, a prosperous young merchant, was seized, bound, beaten, and tortured before being killed. After making a demand for ransom, captors flung his body into San Francisco Bay. Two men, Thomas Thurmond and John Holmes, were arrested and charged with the kidnapping and murder. On November 26, after the corpse had been lifted from the waters, a mob broke into the jail, dragged forth both Thurmond and Holmes, and hanged them in a public square.[4]

In the next year, Mrs. Berry V. Stoll of the Golden State was kidnapped and beaten by her captor who demanded a ransom of $50,000. The ransom was paid and Thomas H. Robinson, Jr., perpetrator of the crime, was caught. Robinson was sentenced by a California court to life imprisonment.

The Karpis-Barker gang was one of the most formidable criminal groups of the 1930s. They didn't hesitate to kill anyone who got in their way while they were robbing banks or mail deliveries. From bank robberies, they turned to kidnapping, taking William Hamm, a millionaire Minnesota brewer, in 1933. His ransom netted the captors $100,000, and shortly after this bonanza they abducted Minnesota banker Edward Bremer, Jr., whose ransom brought them $200,000. Captured in 1936 while in New Orleans, Alvin Karpis served time at the federal prison on Alcatraz Island. Released on parole in 1969, he first went to Canada and from there moved to Spain, where he died from sleeping pills in 1979—an old man and one of the very few major criminals from the Depression Era who did not die a violent death.

The years of the Great Depression produced leaders as well as thousands of ordinary men and women who with indomitable courage and determination overcame hardships not understandable to generations that never witnessed the black horse of real poverty. The Depression Decade also was a period when swindlers, scoundrels, and cheap gangsters made headlines. The two-bit criminal might be a burglar, bank robber, or murderer, but through lurid stories in newspapers, and dramatized accounts from Hollywood cameras or weekly radio shows, actual crimes were downplayed and the criminal fictionalized. Usually he was portrayed as wronged by society and committed crimes in efforts to redress mistreatments he had suffered, imaginary or real. At the end of the story, the thug, finally showing a spark of human kindness, would go out with a crescendo, his reputation enshrined in the minds of readers, viewers, or listeners.

Thus it was with Bonnie and Clyde. Clyde Barrow and Bonnie Parker had met in 1930 when she was nineteen and married to another man; Barrow was twenty-one. Soon afterwards Barrow was sent to Eastham State Prison in Texas for burglary. Bonnie Parker smuggled a machine gun to him which he used in an escape, together with Raymond Hamilton and four other prisoners. Barrow's freedom was short lived, for he was captured and sent back to his cell. Paroled in February, 1932, Barrow collected Bonnie, and the two resumed their careers in crime.

In addition to auto theft, burglaries, and bank robberies, the couple was suspected of numerous murders. By the time both were killed, it was judged they had murdered at least thirteen persons. Barrow, for example, was charged with murdering a police officer in Joplin, Missouri, and kidnapping a man and woman in rural Louisiana. He allegedly killed a man at Hillsboro, Texas, and murdered a sheriff and wounded another officer at a shoot-out in Stringtown, Oklahoma. He attempted to murder a deputy at Wharton, Texas, before committing robberies and murders at Abilene, Sherman, and Dallas.

Ivan "Buck" Barrow, Clyde's brother, was released from prison and with his wife, Blanche, joined Clyde's gang, bringing its total membership to five because it now included William Daniel Jones, a young gunman. This gang embarked on a series of bold robberies dominating the news across the country. They escaped capture in various encounters with the law before police surrounded them in Iowa on July 29, 1933. Buck Barrow was fatally wounded, and his wife Blanche was captured in this melee. Jones, often mistaken for another petty gangster named "Pretty Boy" Floyd, was caught and arrested in Houston in November of that year. Meanwhile, Bonnie and Clyde continued their spree.

In early April, 1934, an FBI agent near Ruston, Louisiana, obtained information that Bonnie and Clyde were hiding out in the vicinity. Accordingly, on May 23rd of that year, a posse, including Texas Ranger Frank Hamer, who had been humiliated by the fugitive pair in a former encounter, was staked out along the highway near Arcadia, Louisiana. Just before dawn, Bonnie and Clyde drove up in a stolen auto, and when they tried to drive away from the blockade they were shot numerous times and died almost instantly.

Folklore subsequently glorified the two criminals as Robin-Hood-like characters, and a 1967 hit movie starring the beautiful and glamorous Fay Dunaway and Warren Beatty was filmed. The real Bonnie and Clyde bore little resemblance to such popular stories.[5]

Similar fictions were wrapped around the career of John Dillinger, another notorious bank robber of mid-western America during the early thirties. Christened John Herbert Dillinger soon after his birth near Indianapolis, Indiana in 1903, young Dillinger was raised by a reportedly strict father and unforgiving stepmother. Dillinger quit school when a teenager, worked briefly in a machine shop, and joined the navy for a few months before deserting and being given a dishonorable discharge. Imprisoned on a burglary charge, he learned the ropes of bank robbery from two hardened robbers and fellow inmates—Harry Pierpont and Russell Clark. The three planned bank heists they intended to commit after being released.

Dillinger was associated with gangs believed to have robbed banks of more than $300,000 before he was captured and sent to jail at the federal penitentiary in Michigan City, Indiana. Paroled from there, within three months he was back in jail at Lima, Ohio. Freed from the Ohio jail with the help of gang members in a breakout during which a guard was killed, the fugitives fled to Tucson, Arizona. Captured there with other gang members, Dillinger was brought back to Crown Point, Indiana, where he was jailed again and charged with murder of a police officer in nearby East Chicago, Indiana.

Using a fake gun made from either wood or soap (accounts differ) and blackened with shoe polish, Dillinger escaped from the Crown Point jail and continued to rob banks. Because he had crossed state lines, the Federal Bureau of Investigation got into his case, and the Department of Justice offered a reward of $20,000 for his capture or $5,000 for information leading to it.

In March, 1934, the FBI got word that Dillinger and cohorts were holed up at Little Bohemia, a summer resort fifty miles north of Rhinelander, Wisconsin. J. Edgar Hoover, Chief of the FBI in Washington, called in reporters and told them his men had the nefarious outlaw surrounded; reporters should be ready for some good news.

As agents moved closer to the building in Little Bohemia where Dillinger and cronies were relaxing, a dog started barking. The criminals were alerted, but the agents were ready. When three Civilian Conservation workers, who had just finished a drink at the bar, got in their car and attempted to drive away, the agents let loose a barrage of fire, killing one man and wounding the other two. Meanwhile, Dillinger and his whole gang escaped unharmed through the back window. The whole affair at Little Bohemia had been a debacle for the FBI.[6]

Capturing John Dillinger had become an obsession with J. Edgar Hoover, Director of the Federal Bureau of Investigation in Washington, D.C. When Dillinger in 1934 went into hiding in Chicago, FBI agents got unimpeachable evidence he was somewhere in the city. Agent Melvin Purvis and his partner learned that Dillinger was dating a woman who was a friend of Anna Sage, a pseudonym for a brothel madam in Gary, Indiana.

It was standard practice for urban police departments to seek information on wanted criminals from known prostitutes, pimps, and madams. The White Slave Traffic Act of 1910—better known by the name of the Illinois congressman who introduced it, James Robert Mann—was aimed at foreign-born madams managing bordellos in the U.S. Madams and each of the "girls" in the establishment were questioned to determine true names, places of birth, business histories, and procurers' identities. Such information was duly reported to FBI headquarters in Washington, D.C. where it became a part of the master files.

In July 1934, one of the regular madams on the FBI's list of informants was Ana Cumpanas, who went by the name Anna Sage. Having been born in Romania and now facing deportation as an undesirable alien, Sage offered Melvin Purvis, the FBI's chief officer in Chicago, a deal. She said John Dillinger, the nation's Public Enemy Number One at the time and with a price of $10,000 on his head, was seeing one of her regulars named Polly Hamilton. Sage promised to lead agents to Dillinger in exchange for the reward money and cancellation of deportation charges against her.

Purvis accepted her offer, and the next night Sage called him, saying she, Polly, and Dillinger were going to a movie. No, she wasn't sure which movie, but most likely it would be either the *Biograph* or the *Marbro*. Purvis had cleared the action with J. Edgar Hoover in Washington, and quickly got his forces to surround the two theaters. Only two men could identify Sage: Sergeant Martin Zarkovich, who had been the FBI's link to the madam, and Melvin Purvis who had met and promised to meet her demands. Zarkovich and several other agents went to the *Marbro*; Purvis waited in a car parked across the street from the *Biograph*.

John Herbert Dillinger's last day on earth was July 22, 1934, when he attended a movie, *Manhattan Melodrama,* at the Biograph Theatre in the Lincoln Park neighborhood of Chicago. Sage had told Purvis that she and a companion were likely to go to a movie that night with Dillinger, and she would wear an agreed-upon "orange dress." Under lights of the movie theater's marquee, the orange dress appeared red. When the movie let out, Purvis stood by watching the front door and by lighting a cigar signaled Dillinger's exit.

Seeing Purvis and other agents, Dillinger jumped in front of his two companions and bolted for a nearby alley, drawing his own pistol from its shoulder holster. By this time he was under fire from a number of guns. He was struck three times, twice in the chest and once by a bullet entering the back of his neck before coming out just under his right eye. Although an ambulance was summoned, it was clear John Dillinger had died almost instantly from his several wounds.[7]

Before his death, legends had begun to circulate about John Dillinger, and the shoot-out set up by the mysterious "lady in red" fueled even more fiction. Screen actor Humphrey Bogart came through with a thinly-disguised Dillinger as the vicious gang leader Duke Mantee in *The Petrified Forest*; another Hollywood actor, Lawrence Tierney, played the title role in a dramatized filming of Dillinger's career. In 1973, in keeping with anti-hero themes then popular, a third movie entitled simply *Dillinger* was released. A movie named *The Lady in Red* was released in 1979, and in a parody of Dillinger's escape from Crown Point, film star Woody Allen shaped the gun from a bar of soap, blackened it with shoe polish only to find that his "weapon" turned to soap suds when it rained.

Kidnappers, assassins, gangsters, and other criminals chose victims from nurseries, businesses, society, or politics. Usually it was a matter of which would be most lucrative, but at times the motive was a vengeful, different opinion; the murder of Senator Huey P. Long had been an example of that.

Not all the news in the thirties was about murders, for in addition to those and gangster exploits, there were other careers reported in detail by newspaper and radio journalists. One career was that of Samuel Insull, an American public utilities financier born in London. Insull migrated to the U.S. in 1881 and first was employed as a private secretary to Thomas A. Edison. By 1907 he had joined with Edison in overcoming competing utilities companies in Chicago. Soon Insull-Edison operations were controlling interurban lines including: the North Shore Line, South Shore Line, Chicago, Aurora, and Elgin lines, and rapid transit lines, which later became the Chicago Rapid Transit Company.

The mammoth interlocking company headed by Insull operated more than three hundred steam plants, two hundred hydroelectric generating plants, and numerous other power industries throughout the United States. The companies flourished, but in 1932 Insull went to Greece and then Turkey before being extradited in 1934 to the United States, where he faced charges of fraud and embezzlement. Insull was acquitted in three separate security fraud trials in the mid-thirties, dominating the headlines during each of them. Broken by exhausting court trials and the Great Depression, Insull, literally penniless, retired to France, where he died of a heart attack in a Paris subway station on July 16, 1938. Historians seemed to agree that most likely Insull was chosen as a scapegoat for financial woes then sweeping the country.[8]

CHAPTER 9: RACIAL STIRRINGS

During WW I and its immediate aftermath, hundreds of thousands of negroes* in the South had migrated to the North, drawn there by high wages and job openings in mill or factory. In the sixty years following the close of the Civil War, subservience of negroes throughout the South was unquestioned. Arson, whippings, kidnappings, and worse against blacks were common and rarely investigated. Much of the disturbance could be traced to gangs of white, hooded mobsters who termed themselves the Ku Klux Klan. Many attacks were by unmasked local citizens, determined "to keep nigras in their place." The cult of violence spread, and during the 1920s throughout the North and Midwest as well as the South, the Ku Klux Klan incited violence against Catholics, Jews, Asiatics, or whatever minority could be considered different.

At the start of the Great Depression and as it worsened, the targets of discrimination began suffering first—none more so than negroes. Most authorities agree that, in 1933, more than twice as many negroes as whites were on relief. Sociology Professor Charles S. Johnson reported: "Nearly half the negro working African-Americans population in New York was on relief."[1]

Despite discriminations and hardships throughout the Great Depression, World War II helped usher in a change of attitudes toward blacks, and very slowly more respect for the race began to surface.

A book published just before the close of World War II gave an unbiased opinion of race relations in America. Gunnar Myrdal, a distinguished Swedish economist, author of the study *An American Dilemma: the Negro Problem and Modern Democracy* painstakingly detailed what he saw as obstacles to the full participation in American society faced by African-Americans in the '30s and early '40s. Myrdal described the circle in which whites oppressed blacks, and then pointed to poor performance by blacks as reason for the oppression. The only solution, he argued, was to cure whites of their prejudice or improve the circumstances in which blacks

*An earlier note explained that in the years being reported in this narrative, the terms negro or colored were preferred. The generic nouns "Afro-Americans" and "blacks" did not come into popularity until well after the end of World War II.

lived, which then would disprove the whites' preconceived notions. Myrdal's en-cyclopedic study concluded that the "negro problem" was a "white man's prob-lem." Collectively, whites were responsible for the disadvantageous situations in which blacks were trapped.[2]

Influenced by Myrdal and other writers who echoed his findings, the status of blacks in American society slowly began to improve. Even prior to that time, in-dividual blacks in the face of great odds had made names for themselves. There was Booker T. Washington not long after the Civil War, scientist George Washing-ton Carver a bit later, then W. E. B. DuBois and Roy Wilkins in the 1930s and 1940s. Wilkins would be criticized by militant blacks more militant than he, but as the head of the Railway Porters' Union there is little doubt he could have been a worthy presidential candidate if he had not been black.

During hard times the plight of minorities is particularly onerous, and when crimes are committed blame readily falls upon them. In the Deep South of the 1930s, jurors were quick to convict blacks if they happened to be even near the scene where a crime had been committed. One of the most shameful examples of such injustices can be seen in the drawn-out case of the Scottsboro Boys.

Few crimes in American history produced as many trials, convictions, rever-sals, and retrials as did an alleged gang rape of two white girls by nine black teenagers on a southern railroad freight run on March 25, 1931. Riding freight trains was common during those lean years of the Depression, and on a particular train en route to Memphis were nine black youths and four young whites, two males and two females. Soon after crossing the Alabama border, a fight between blacks and whites broke out, and the whites were forced off the train. They went to the nearest stationmaster and said they had been assaulted by a gang of blacks. A white posse was immediately assembled, and when the train pulled into Steven-son, Alabama, the posse rushed it, capturing every black aboard. The nine black teenagers were tied together, loaded on a truck, and taken to nearby Scottsboro.

Among the posse members were two millworkers, Victoria Price and Ruby Bates, who said they had been raped by a gang of twelve blacks armed with pistols and knives. In the first trial, the Scottsboro Boys, as they had been dubbed, were defended by lawyers who proved to be far less competent than the prosecutors. One of the indicted boys was less than twelve years old. The defense offered only the defendants themselves as witnesses, and often the testimonies were rambling, incoherent, and riddled with obvious misstatements. Neither Ruby Bates nor Vic-toria Price was questioned about contradictions in their testimonies, and no closing arguments were advanced by defense attorneys.

Eight of the nine Scottsboro Boys were convicted and sentenced to death. A mistrial was declared in the case against twelve-year-old Roy Wright when only eleven of the twelve jurors agreed to vote the death penalty for such a young person.

The cases were appealed, and in January, 1932, the Alabama Supreme Court af-firmed all but one of the eight convictions and death sentences. Next, the cases were ap-pealed to the U.S. Supreme Court, which overturned all the convictions, ruling that the right of the defendants under the Fourteenth Amendment's due process clause competent legal counsel had been denied; there would have to be new trials.

By the time the next trial began, the International Labor Defense organization, the legal arm of the Communist Party, had joined the arguments, hoping to make the case a recruiting tool among southern blacks and northern liberals. Throughout the trials, the Communist Party in America threw its support behind the defense and shamelessly exploited the case in its propaganda.

The International Labor Defense hired Samuel Liebowitz, a mainline Democrat and one of New York's most famous criminal lawyers, to defend the boys. Liebowitz himself was no Communist but was assisted by the ILD's chief attorney. The stew bubbled even more with ingredients of law, race, and politics. The Scottsboro Boys spent the two years between their first trials and the second round in the deplorable conditions of Depression-era Alabama prisons.

The second trial opened in the courtroom of Judge James Horton, and Leibowitz immediately moved to quash the indictments on grounds that negroes had been systemically excluded from jury rolls. He raised more hackles when he insisted that the prosecutor stop his practice of calling black witnesses by their first names. Local observers expected that an attorney would defend rapists—that was part of the American justice system—but to come to Alabama and attack social patterns was unforgivable. As expected, the motion to quash the indictment was denied.

Leibowitz called Victoria Price to the stand, and his cross-examination of her was merciless. He was able to establish that she was a prostitute and had lain with other men two days before the alleged gang attack. Semen from at least two of the other white men was found in her vagina.

Dr. R. R. Bridges, the doctor who examined the two girls less than two hours after the alleged rape, testified that both girls were calm, composed, free of bleeding, and showed no vaginal damage. The semen that Dr. Bridges found in the two girls was non-motile—i.e. inert or dead—and jurors learned that semen usually lived from twelve to forty-eight hours after intercourse.

Defense lawyers were able to prove there had been no boardinghouse that Victoria Price said she had owned, and that she had lied numerous other times while giving testimony. One of the accused boys was shown to have been suffering from venereal disease at the time of the alleged rape and so weak that he could not walk without a cane, let alone leap from boxcar to boxcar as Price had claimed. Prosecutor Thomas Knight, Jr. asked one of the accused boys, Ozzie Powell, "Ozzie, how much schooling have you had in your life?" The boy replied, "About three months."

Lester Carter, one of the defense's most spectacular witnesses, had been the white traveling companion of Price and Bates. Carter testified that he and Jack Tiller, a regular trick for Victoria Price, had made love to the two whores in a hobo jungle at Huntsville, Alabama, the night before the four left on the freight train.

Final witness for the defense was Ruby Bates, who had been in hiding since the first trial. Under probing questions, Bates said she had a troubled conscience and that noted New York minister Harry Emerson Fosdick had encouraged her "to tell the truth about what happened on March 25, 1931." There had been no rape; none of the accused had touched either her or Price. Price had persuaded her to "frame up" the story in order to avoid any chance of being prosecuted under the

Mann Act, a law which provided heavy penalties for crossing state lines for immoral purposes.

During summations made in this trial, one of the prosecutors asked, "Is justice in this case going to be bought and sold with Jew money from New York?" Leibowitz jumped up and immediately asked for a mistrial, which the judge refused to declare. This second trial ended on April 8, 1933, when jurors quickly returned a verdict pronouncing Patterson guilty with a sentence of death.

Two months later, defense attorneys presented another motion for a third trial. Judge James Horton, the same presiding officer over the trial that had found Patterson guilty, heard the motions. In interims between trials, Judge Horton had become convinced that Price was lying, and with corroboration from private sources he stunned listeners in the courtroom of Athens, his hometown, by setting aside the guilty verdict and ordering a new trial.

The prosecution succeeded in getting this third attempt transferred out of Horton's jurisdiction, and a new presiding officer, Judge William Callahan, was assigned. In the third trial, a prosecution witness, although differing in details, corroborated most of Victoria Price's testimony. However, defense lawyers showed that the prosecution had sent money to the witness's mother, and they contended that now the prosecutors were calling in their chips. Nevertheless, guilty verdicts were again returned, but Judge Callahan agreed to postpone further trials until other appeals still pending had run their course.

It was February 1935 before the U.S. Supreme Court heard arguments that the Alabama convictions should be overturned because blacks there had been excluded from jury rolls. Six weeks later the Court unanimously ruled the Alabama trials had been unconstitutional, thus setting aside the earlier convictions.

In a fourth trial begun in January 1936 and held before the same Judge William Callahan, one defendant, Haywood Patterson, was again found guilty, but his sentence of death was changed to a compromise of seventy-five years in prison. It was the first time in the history of Alabama that a black man convicted of raping a white woman had not been sentenced to death.

Another trial was held before Judge Callahan in July 1937, and in this confrontation three of the original nine defendants were again convicted; another four were either exonerated or given parole. Eventually all of the nine Scottsboro Boys found their way out of Alabama prisons, but stories of their ordeals remain a shameful episode in the nation's history. The accounts make clear that at least in the Deep South during the 1930s, a black man charged with raping a white woman was not given the usual presumption of innocence until proved guilty. He was believed guilty until and unless he could prove innocence beyond all reasonable doubt.

It would be unfair to look at the Scottsboro case and condemn the whole South. The region had many honest and courageous white men and women. Look at the career of Judge James Horton. It was he who in the face of overwhelming criticism from neighbors with whom he lived set aside the conviction of one defendant and ordered a new trial despite the consequences that decision would have on his own career. Defeated in the next election, his actions showed heroism, pure and simple.[3]

No entity suffered from discrimination as much as the blacks, and all too often some were lynched by hate-crazed mobs. It is virtually impossible to determine exactly how many blacks were subjected to this bestial practice because so many of these incidents went unreported or law enforcement officials did not investigate them; however, the Tuskegee Institute, in a conservative estimate, put the figure of 3,436 blacks lynched between the years of 1882 and 1950.[4]

Nor were all the hangings in the South. Racial discrimination was prevalent in states of the Midwest, and nowhere more than in central and northern Indiana. On a hot summer night in 1930, a white lynch mob stormed the county jail in Marion, Indiana, and seized two inmates, Thomas Shipp, eighteen, and Abram Smith, nineteen. The two young black men had been arrested that afternoon in connection with the shooting death of a white man and the rape of his girlfriend.

The mob broke into the jail, carried the prisoners out of their cells, and dragged them to a tree at the corner of the jailhouse. Ropes were put around the neck of each of the two young prisoners and ends of the ropes slung over a limb eight feet from the ground. Still protesting their innocence and without benefit of trial or even a hearing, the two black youths were hanged. Spectators numbered twenty-two persons, some laughing and smiling, and some expressionless. One man with a tattooed forearm pointed toward the dangling bodies, and a young man in a white shirt held the hand of a girl in a summer dress; both are smiling into the camera. Watchers of the grisly scene looked "as placid as rubes at a stock show."[5] Newspaper pictures years thereafter would show Marion, Indiana's ugliest hour.

Blacks suffered most, but other minorities were also targeted by hate groups. Foremost among attackers was the Ku Klux Klan. The name, rituals, and attitudes of the original Ku Klux Klan lay in an organization incorporated in the year 1915 in the State of Georgia. The name the new society chose was Invisible Empire, Knights of the Ku Klux Klan, and its membership was open to native-born, white, Protestant males, sixteen years of age or older. Blacks, Roman Catholics, and Jews were excluded and were increasingly made targets of defamation and persecution.

Immediately following WW I, the Ku Klux Klan expanded rapidly, extending well beyond the South. Although white supremacy remained a core issue throughout the 1920s, the Klan also mounted attacks on those it considered to be outside aliens, particularly the Roman Catholic Church, which it believed was threatening traditional American values. Non-Protestants, aliens, liberals, trade unionists and striking workers were denounced as subversives.

Klan members burned crosses to frighten citizens, and masked Klansmen marched through streets, carrying placards threatening various persons with punishments and warning others to leave town. Individuals were kidnapped, flogged, or mutilated by the Klan, and some victims were lynched or murdered. Few prosecutions of Klansmen resulted, and in several communities the culprits were abetted by local officials.

The peak of membership in the Ku Klux Klan was in the mid-1920s, when estimates put the number at over three million. In 1924 the Klan practically took over Indiana; favorite targets in that state then were alcohol and adultery. Demise of the Ku Klux Klan in the Hoosier State came quickly when David Stephenson,

"Grand Dragon" in the state and a leader who had reaped millions from membership fees and sales of nightshirts, was convicted of raping a young woman and causing her death.

CHAPTER 10: LABOR UNIONS

Organized labor in America passed through several phases, much as it had done in Europe, before it attained enough power to meet established capital on equal terms.

In coal mining sections of Pennsylvania, disputes led by the Molly Maguires broke out a decade after the close of the nation's Civil War. The Molly Maguires, composed mainly of Irish Catholics, roamed the countryside burning private property, controlling county officials, and frequently murdering bosses or supervisors who offended them. Ten Molly Maguire murderers were brought to trial in 1877; their hangings marked the end of Molly Maguire organizations.

Roughly in the same period, early labor organizations in America had been outgrowths of groups of printers, carpenters, tailors, weavers, and others closely linked craft workers whose purpose was to keep up standards and to prevent the hiring by employers of untrained persons. Of the first national unions, the Knights of Labor, founded in 1869, was the most important, but within a decade of its birth was challenged by the American Federation of Labor, led by Samuel Gompers. The A. F. of L. was strictly a craft union, meaning its members had to be workers already skilled in a specific trade.

Eugene V. Debs from Terre Haute, Indiana, in 1893, launched a labor organization much wider than established trade unions. His American Railway Union aimed to include all railroad workers—skilled or otherwise. In May 1894, a single year after Debs' union got started, one of the most memorable strikes in U.S. history took place in Pullman, Illinois, a suburb which within five years would become part of the city of Chicago. Protests against wage cuts for railroad workers there erupted into a strike, and the American Railway Union organized a supporting boycott. There was sharp dispute between Illinois Governor John P. Altgeld and U.S. President Grover Cleveland over the sending in of federal troops to quell the disturbance. President Cleveland prevailed, and with federal uniformed troops on the scene, the strike was broken within six weeks. Debs, leader of the Railway Union, was charged with contempt of court and imprisoned for six months at Woodstock, Illinois.

In 1904, Debs became head of the Socialist party and ran on that party's ticket for the U.S. Presidency in both 1908 and 1912. Socialists refused to take part in government war efforts in the First World War, and, in 1918, Debs, a leading pacifist, was sentenced to ten-year imprisonment for speaking in violation of the Espionage Act. Though still in a federal prison, in 1920 he again ran for the presidency and from his Atlanta jail cell polled nearly a million votes.[1]

Shortly before the New Deal Administration in 1933 took office, the Norris-LaGuardia Act was blocking federal courts from interfering on behalf of employers. The Norris-LaGuardia Act left management and labor unions free to bring economic pressure in collective-bargaining practices upon each other as best they could. Provisions in the law forbade courts to issue injunctions against most ordinary collective-bargaining practices, and it made unenforceable any yellow-dog contracts—i.e. pledges from employees that they would *not* join unions.

In the hard times of the 1930s, work stoppages across America broke out like freckles beneath a Kansas sun. Longshoremen and other dock workers on the U.S. Pacific and Atlantic coasts engaged in strikes, marked by violence and fatalities. A strike of San Francisco dock workers in July 1934 flared briefly but was ended by arbitration that same month. A month later, a more prolonged stoppage occurred when strike orders issued by the United Textile Workers of America to more than 1,000,000 employees in the cotton, silk, and wool divisions went into effect. The trouble was greatest in Georgia, South Carolina, Southern North Carolina, and in Maine and Rhode Island. Twenty persons were killed when the National Guard and mobs clashed in several states. President Franklin Roosevelt's personal appeal ended the strike on September 22, 1934, and negotiations between the two adversaries were resumed.

The Depression spawned schisms, though, within the labor movement, and at the American Federation of Labor convention in 1935, burly John L. Lewis, a member of the AFL Executive Council, led fellow unionists in demanding that the Federation grant unrestricted charters to whatever new locals desired them. His plea meant an industrial-wide union, rather than just narrow craft unions, and if granted would diminish the powers of recognition practiced by entrenched craftsmen. The Executive Council of the AFL promised to act on Lewis's demands, but the promise was not fulfilled. At the Federation's convention the following year a roll call on the issue showed 40 percent of the members agreed with Lewis.

On November 9, 1935, shortly after the convention for that year, Lewis and his bloc of supporters had taken the first step in forming the Committee for Industrial Organization (CIO). Goals of the CIO were: improvement in hours and wages, securing the closed shop, and establishing that union's right to represent workers in collective bargaining. Under the aggressive leadership of Lewis, the CIO set out to unionize workers in steel, automobile, textile, and public utilities—entities whose executives heretofore had refused to deal with established labor unions. The new union aimed to draw into its ranks all workers, unskilled and semi-skilled, within an industry—steel, automobile, textile, and public utilities. Under such broadened appeal, the CIO signed up hundreds of thousands of laborers and was supported by "white-collar" sympathizers from journalism and other business interests.

Renewed fears of Bolshevism broke out when strikes began appearing every-where—in the building trades, among longshoremen, shipyard men, stockyard workers, carpenters, shoe workers, telephone men, and so *ad infinitum*. Most of the strikers were American unionists whose lives and families were being threatened by uncaring employers, but strikers also included a rag-tag-and-bobtail collection of anarchists and communists—many of whom were foreign born. Some of the latter had watched the Revolution in Russia and now took their goals directly from Moscow.

Admittedly, this group was a tiny minority—absurdly narrow if one considers the tremendous fuss they caused—but poverty is fertile ground for radicalism. The excessive zeal and unconstitutional acts of U. S. Attorney General A. Mitchell Palmer in attempting to halt the Red Menace of the twenties had become familiar history; yet, as poverty spread during the early nineteen thirties strikes and labor unrest erupted.

The CIO won a sensational victory over the steel industry if one considered defeats unions had suffered in the infamous Homestead Strike of 1892 and in the nation-wide strike of 1919, but the two-billion dollar United States Steel Corpo-ration, hoping to repeat earlier triumphs, led industrial-wide efforts to break up union meetings, to create "citizen movements" designed to promote an atmosphere of unreason and fear, and to use local presses for the purpose of instilling fear of Communist infiltrations.

The CIO struck back, and in waging contests with employers it initiated acts called "sit-downs," during which employees would move onto company premises but refuse to work until their demands had been met. Some employers surrendered; other big corporations, such as Republic Steel and General Motors, went to court seeking rescue of their property. Courts responded with a series of injunctions, and when workers resisted the orders, violence resulted.

In the year Franklin Roosevelt began his second administration, John L. Lewis was in the peak of glory. Triumphs of the CIO under his aggressive leadership had brought firm after firm into compliance until rolls of the new union totaled 30,000 contracts and more than three million workers. Moreover, organized labor now extended beyond working class wards; members included college students, office staffs, journalists, store clerks, and even a union of clergymen.

There was no denying the bargaining power of both craft and industrial unions, but by the middle of the decade, resentment against labor spread as results of in-numerable strikes. In May 1937, Lewis took his men out—70,000 workers in 27 factories. Management of steel companies under strike retaliated by spending more than $4,000,000 in expanding company police and hiring more armed watchmen and related employees. Strikebreakers were shielded while entering or leaving the plants and, while inside at work, they were fed by parcel post and parachute drops.

This strike was still unsettled when elsewhere violence came on Memorial Day. In what most newspapers were quick to call a "massacre," open warfare broke out in South Chicago. The confrontation occurred near shops of the Republic Steel Company. Strikers there tried to form picket lines outside the company's gates, and police were summoned. Five hundred heavily armed Chicago policemen amassed in direct contravention of Mayor Edward Kelly's order that a peaceful demonstration would be permitted. As a parade of strikers and supporters edged toward the mill, the policemen, some of whom were armed with Browning 30-caliber machine guns, blocked their passage.

Two hundred and fifty yards in front of gates to the mill, a wedge of bluecoats, yanking revolvers free and swinging nightsticks, lit into the approaching walkers, including women and children. Tempers rose, and provocations later cited by the police took place as marchers called out taunts. A few empty pop bottles were thrown, and at that point, police grenades began to fly. A pall of nauseous tear gas settled over the crowd; women and children screamed as they fled, and the parade buckled and broke.

Shots from the police began, the first of which were scattered, but as the melee continued the uniformed men fired volleys. Picketing protesters lay on the grass or crawled about aimlessly. In the violence of the confrontation, ten people were killed and forty wounded.

Paramount newsreels filmed it all but suppressed the films, giving the fatuous explanation that showing them might incite riot. The *St. Louis Post-Dispatch* printed accounts of the incident, but the *Chicago Tribune* alleged that walkers came to the plant organized and "lusting for blood." Both the McCormick and Hearst press branded the debacle as "communistic inspired," and no one was ever prosecuted.

From a subsequent U. S. Congressional investigation, Wisconsin Senator Robert M. LaFollette, Jr. summarized his committee's findings:

...provocation for the police assault did not go beyond abusing language and the throwing of isolated missiles from the rear ranks of the marchers . . . . From all the evidence, we think it plain that the force employed by the police was far in excess of that which the occasion required. Its use must be ascribed either to gross inefficiency in the performance of police duty, or a deliberate attempt to intimidate the strikers.[2]

Workers of the nation said they were tired of waiting for corporation industry to right their economic wrongs, to alleviate their social agony, and to grant them their political rights. Despairing of fair treatment, they resolved to do something for themselves, so sit-down strikes continued to spread despite their illegality. When workers adopted the tactic at General Motors in Detroit, the Governor of Michigan refused to send in state troopers; instead, he urged further negotiations. There was an impasse of six weeks before the GM strike ended, and the UAW was acknowledged as the sole bargaining agency for its members.

Organized labor had thrown its weight to the candidacy of FDR in 1932, and by 1934 labor organizations were lined up solidly behind his party. FDR had been so sure of labor's vote he had not even accepted an invitation from the Democratic National Committee's Labor Division to make a major campaign speech under its auspices.

Successful in confrontations with General Motors and U. S. Steel companies, John L. Lewis, head of United Mine Workers of America, had left the Republican

Party and turned New Dealer, providing Democrats with more than a half-million dollars in campaign funds. By 1936, when Roosevelt was failing to heed all of Lewis's demands, the union leader was ready to take on the president.

From his position as the nation's Chief Executive, Roosevelt had followed the disturbances, and in a moment of petulance over the never-ending arguments between labor and management declared "a plague on both your houses."

The "plague" statement so angered Lewis, who personally hated FDR but had thrown full support of the United Mine Workers to him, now laid the cutting lash of oratory on "that man in the White House." In Washington, D.C., on September 3, 1937, Lewis spoke to miners and the nation, giving an address called "Labor and the Nation." In sermonic voice, Lewis indicted the President.

Labor, like Israel, has many sorrows. Its women weep for their fallen, and they lament for the future of the children of the race. It ill-behooves one who has supped at labor's table and who has been sheltered in labor's house to curse with equal fervor and with fine impartiality both labor and its adversaries when they become locked in deadly embrace.[3]

The CIO was successful in organizing the United Automobile Workers of America. Just as in steel industries, automotive plants utilized measures of repression, espionage, and intimidation against union organizers, but workers eventually prevailed. In the Fisher Body Plant in Cleveland, when workers refused to leave company premises, production was halted; not even a court injunction could dislodge the defiant men.

Public opinion was turning against tactics of the militant CIO, however, and the unruly disturbances forced congressional action. One of the last New Deal reform measures, the Fair Labor Standards Act, was introduced early in 1937 and passed by Congress in June of the following year. The Act, drawn by Senator Hugo Black of Alabama, provided for a forty-cent hourly minimum, set a maximum work week of forty hours, with time and a half for overtime, and banned labor for children under sixteen.

The new measure slowed, yet did not halt, all labor unrest. Over 688,000 men went out on strike in 1937. In 1939, despite improvements brought by the Fair Labor Standard Act, the figure soared to over 1,170,000.

The Fair Labor Standards Act was challenged legally but sustained by a unanimous decision when it reached the U.S. Supreme Court. President Roosevelt called the law "the most far-reaching, far-sighted program for the benefit of workers ever adopted in this or any other country."[4]

Chapter 11: Entry of Franklin Roosevelt

The political history of the United States in the ten years between 1930 and 1940 might well be called the era of Franklin D. Roosevelt. True, he was not elected President until November, 1932, but wheels pushing him toward that office had begun turning much earlier.

The 1880s was an age of moguls—an age that displayed poverty and wealth, unrest and stability—an age when thousands of unemployed workers searched for jobs, bread, and shelter while a few fortunate others built half-million-dollar yachts and sumptuous mansions. Horatio Alger's rags-to-riches writings encouraged entrepreneurs, and mainly because there were vast natural resources and unsettled territories, there was just enough evidence to buttress his thesis.

The Scottish immigrant Andrew Carnegie, Colossus of Pittsburgh, had amassed millions through manufacturing steel, and Cornelius Vanderbilt had made a fortune in steamboats; his descendants added to their founder's enormous wealth. The Vanderbilts lived in a fifty-four-room Renaissance mansion a few miles to the north of where Franklin Roosevelt was born, but despite the wealth started by Cornelius and enlarged by his son W. H. Vanderbilt, Franklin's father would always consider the Vanderbilts as *nouveau riche,* yet to be accepted in the best levels of society.

For the majority of Americans at the time, the economic picture was not so rosy. The average income of eleven million out of the twelve million American families was slightly less than $400 a year, and in eastern cities were slums, sweatshops, crowded tenements, and unemployed workers.

The Delano and Roosevelt families in New York State had no firsthand knowledge of poverty. On the Delano side, a Flemish seafarer, Philippe de la Noy Delano, had settled in Massachusetts very early in the seventeenth century. The first Roosevelt—Claes Martenszen van Roosevelt—came from Holland to New Amsterdam in 1613. The descendants of these two progenitors married so consistently with English families in New England that future generations would become ever more English in orientation and outlook.

James Roosevelt—the great-great-great grandson of Claes Martenszen—was

---

father of Franklin Delano Roosevelt. After the death of his first wife, James had married Sara Delano, aged twenty-six, and Franklin would be the only child born to the couple.

Sara once described Franklin's arrival:

[He] . . . was plump, and nice . . . born right here in this house; one never went to hospitals in those days . . . I realize how much more scientific hospital care is today, but I am old-fashioned enough to think it's nicer for a baby to be born in his own home. I've passed the door of that sunny, upstairs room many hundreds of times in my long life, and oh! So often I've remembered that there my son first saw the light of day . . .[1]

All accounts picture Franklin Roosevelt as a bright, handsome, and happy infant. Constantly in the company of an adoring, watchful mother and surrounded by servants, he entered a boyhood that had few rivals if measured by comforts, travel, security, formal training—all the privileges enjoyed at the time by the few families with wealth and high social position. Franklin was taken to Europe for the first time when he was three, and thereafter he spent a few months of each year abroad. In the course of his boyhood, he had a series of nurses, governesses, and tutors—seven different ones by the time he was fourteen—and at that age his mother enrolled him at Groton, a private school in Massachusetts.

From Groton, Franklin went to Harvard, following the path of other boys in his economic and social class. At Harvard, he was an average student, getting grades seldom above a B and failing in several examinations. Nevertheless, he graduated from Harvard and then went to Columbia University, where he studied law from 1904 to 1907.

After gaining admission to the bar of New York State, Roosevelt left Columbia without graduating and joined a well-established law firm. His three-year practice of law was "more or less casual," and in 1910 he opted for active politics. Departing from the Republican fold of his cousin Theodore, Franklin ran a colorful and successful campaign for the New York Senate.

Not all Tammany leaders were pleased to welcome the handsome, young aristocrat into their ranks. Among incoming members of the Assembly at Albany, "Big Tim" Sullivan, political boss of the party in the Bowery, when first spotting Franklin speaking in cultured language, cigarette holder held firmly in his mouth, and gold pince-nez glasses across his nose, is supposed to have said, "Well, if we've caught a Roosevelt, we'd better take him down and drop him off the dock."[2]

Franklin Roosevelt served in the New York Senate from 1911 until 1913, and in the latter year President Woodrow Wilson appointed him assistant secretary of the navy, a post he held for the next seven years. Roosevelt's unwavering support of the Democratic national leadership won him the vice-presidential nomination on the losing Cox ticket in 1920.

A year later, a sudden and severe attack of polio at his summer home in Campobello, New Brunswick, left him apparently a hopeless invalid, but during the next seven years he fought his way back to health, used his leisure for study and correspondence, and emerged from forced retirement no longer just a likeable, wealthy playboy, but a man with deep ambitions.

His political comeback got a major boost at the Democratic National Convention in 1924, where he nominated New York Governor Alfred E. Smith for president. Roosevelt called Smith the "happy warrior of the political battlefield." Delegates at the convention erupted; the applause was deafening, and Roosevelt's concluding sentences were drowned out by shouts of approval. Smith did not win the nomination, and the Democratic nominee, John W. Davis, was defeated by Republican Calvin Coolidge in that November.

Four years afterward, Governor Smith again asked Roosevelt to make the nominating speech. Franklin's speech on this second occasion was good but not as compelling as the "Happy Warrior" one. An outcome, however, came at the New York state convention in 1928 when the Democrats nominated Franklin Roosevelt to succeed Smith as governor of the Empire State. During this race for the governorship, Roosevelt traveled by automobile, which permitted him to stop at crossroads, shake hands, and make a few remarks. His campaigning was so vigorous that it rebutted any who suggested that his health was not strong enough to hold public office.

As early as midnight on election eve in 1928, it was clear that Democrats were not going to win the presidency, but in New York the race for governor was exceedingly close. Not until the next day did Roosevelt learn that his hard campaigning had brought him a hairbreadth victory. Almost immediately, Governor Roosevelt's closest advisers, led by James Farley and Louis Howe, began developing strategies aimed toward winning the presidential nomination for him in 1932.

By 1930, financiers, banks, and big business had lost respect due to the debacle of '29, yet, despite stories of millionaires and brokers committing suicide, most men and women of wealth had enough to tide them over. Alarms spread rapidly, though, after December 1930, when the Bank of the United States in New York City was closed by order of the State Assembly.[3]

In congressional elections of 1930, Republicans, in their first setback since 1916, lost their majority in the Senate, and in the House their majority shrank from 103 to 2. Two years later the GOP held its convention in Chicago and re-nominated President Hoover and Vice President Charles Curtis. The lethargic gathering produced no surprises, but delegates were confident; they remembered being trounced in 1928 and now were convinced their rivals were badly divided.

Debris left by Republicans in the Chicago Stadium had hardly been swept away before Democrats began arriving. In contrast to the convention just concluded, the Democratic meeting was exuberant, rowdy, and bitter, yet it would become a landmark in the nation's history.

There was a free-for-all battle for the presidential nomination. Al Smith, the party's candidate in 1928, wanted it again. "Cactus Jack" Garner of Texas, Speaker of the House, had sizeable support, and other potential nominees included William MacAdoo (President Woodrow Wilson's son-in-law), Newton D. Baker (Wilson's Secretary of State), Owen D. Young, who had helped engineer a financial recovery for the German Republic, and two governors of U.S. states—Harry F. Byrd of Virginia and "Alfalfa" Bill Murray of Oklahoma. All of them were being challenged by Franklin D. Roosevelt of New York.

One by one the contenders were eliminated, and Roosevelt was named on the fourth ballot with approval from all his opponents except Smith, who, after a period of sulking, finally yielded his valuable support.

Franklin Delano Roosevelt was fifty years old and still considered by many as a wealthy playboy in politics. Walter Lippmann, dean of American journalists for more than thirty years, viewed Roosevelt as a likeable sort of fellow, dismissing him as "an amiable . . . pleasant man who, without any important qualifications for the office, who would very much like to be President."

In truth, Roosevelt in 1932 brought considerable experience to the ticket. He had degrees from three schools: Groton, Harvard, and the Columbia Law School, had tried law practice and business for a couple of years, married Eleanor Roosevelt, niece of his cousin Theodore, whom he greatly admired.

Having supported Woodrow Wilson in 1912, and with being named assistant secretary of the navy, these led to his vice-presidential nomination on the losing Cox ticket in 1920, and his speeches at national conventions in 1924 and 1928 had impressed countless Democratic Party leaders. From the governor's chair in the Empire State, FDR did so well that in 1930 he was re-elected by a whopping 700,000 votes, thus making him a *bona fide* contender for the presidency.

CHAPTER 12: THE BIG CHANGE

When Franklin D. Roosevelt was nominated for the presidency in 1932, he broke the tradition that a nominee should await formal notification of his selection. The morning after receiving that news he charted an airplane and flew from Albany, New York, to Chicago. From aboard the plane during its flight came regular radio reports relayed to an eager public via commercial radio stations. It was drama at a time when everyone was anxious for something—anything—to be done to lift them from their malaise.

Headwinds delayed the plane's flight, and when Roosevelt and his party arrived in Chicago, the airport was crowded with waiting people. As his car sped toward the Stadium, streets of the Windy City were lined with thousands of people—to whom he tipped his hat and shouted "hello," first to one side and then to the other. Inside the hall when he began his acceptance speech, Roosevelt apologized for his lateness by saying, ". . . but I have no control over the winds of Heaven . . ." And in the final paragraph of his speech, he announced his promise:

I pledge you, I pledge myself, to a new deal for the American people. Let us all here assembled constitute ourselves prophets of a new order of competence and of courage. This is more than a political campaign; it is a call to arms. Give me your help, not to win votes alone, but to win in this crusade to restore America to its own people.[1]

Even before he had been nominated, Roosevelt had asked a close adviser, Judge Samuel Rosenman, to draft an acceptance speech. The Judge had come to Albany and had roughed out ideas, including the phrase that would become the trademark of FDR's first administration. In his memoirs, Rosenman wrote:

. . .the peroration I drafted had in it two words to which I gave little thought at the time, but which within a week became accepted as symbolic of the whole new philosophy and program of the Democratic candidate. Intended to epitomize the program of 'bold experimentation' on behalf of the 'forgotten man,' the phrase was in the sentence "I pledge you, I pledge myself, to a **new deal** *[emphasis supplied] for the American people.*[2]

The day after delivery of the acceptance speech, a leading newspaper on its front page printed a cartoon picturing a farmer leaning on his hoe and looking upwards toward an airplane. A buoyant Franklin Roosevelt was in the cockpit, and on the wings of the plane were emblazoned the words: *New Deal.* Thus a two-word phrase was added to the American lexicon, and, at the time, no one suspected the extent to which it would be used.

Throughout the political campaign of 1932, the main difference between the two candidates for the presidency was clear. Hoover wanted to use the powers of the federal government sparingly; Franklin Roosevelt was ready to intervene directly.

Most of the country celebrated the landslide victory of the Democrats that November, but a few diehard conservatives damned the new president as a traitor to his class and waited for prices to fall even lower.

After his win, President-elect Roosevelt went on a vacation cruise in the Caribbean. On February 15, 1933, he came ashore in Miami and was greeted by a crowd of more than 10,000 persons as he sat in an open car talking with Chicago's Mayor Anton Cermak. One spectator climbed on a box amidst the gathering and, taking a pistol from his pocket, fired six shots at the two occupants of the car. A bullet grazed a Secret Service man, and Cermak, struck in the shoulder and chest, slumped to the floor. Roosevelt unhurt, doubled up in his seat for protection, while the enraged crowd converged on the gunman and pummeled him to the ground.

The gunman was Guiseppe Zangara, a thirty-two-year-old unemployed bricklayer from Paterson, New Jersey, who told police, "I hate all Presidents, no matter what country they come from."

The unconscious Cermak was rushed to the nearest hospital where he lingered for three weeks before dying on March 6, 1933. The assassin Zangara was indicted for murder on the same day, pleaded guilty, and was electrocuted in a Florida state prison on March 20th of that year.[3]

Inauguration Day for the incoming President was March 4, 1932, and weather in Washington, D.C. that morning was as dreary as the national mood. A day earlier, two of Franklin Roosevelt's advisers throughout the campaign, Raymond Moley, recognized leader of "idea men," dubbed by many as the *Brain Trust*, and William H. Woodin, designated by the President-elect as secretary of the treasury, went "over to the Treasury . . .[to] see if we can give those fellows there a hand," as Woodin put it.[4]

Woodin and Moley found that nearly all conferees at the Treasury agreed with President Hoover in his commitment to a profit-oriented society, one thoroughly conservative, endorsing "free enterprise" and firm in believing that problems of money and banking were best left in hands of private businessmen and industrialists.

Early the next morning, Moley and Woodin visited their chief in his suite at the Mayflower Hotel across from the White House. FDR listened to the two's account of their conversations at Treasury; then he heartily approved of what they had said and done.

In that bleak year of 1932, banks throughout the nation had started failing, posing dreadful threats to the middle and upper classes. By March, newspaper headlines reported the dire happenings and outstripped by far any reader interest in darkening reports from abroad. Millions of depositors lost part or all of their savings. Shaky banks were overrun by nervous depositors, and by executive orders more than half the states in the Union had closed all banks within their territories. Rumors spread that even in Chicago and New York, the nation's two largest cities, there were such debilitating drains that continued functioning of banks there was doubtful. Across America, wheels of industry and commerce were grinding to a stop; a total paralysis of the entire economy was imminent.

After Moley and Woodin had given their report, FDR asked them if they had any recommendations. The two had come prepared. The new president, they said, in one of his very first moves should invoke the powers of the Trading with the Enemy Act and declare a national bank holiday. Secondly, the president should call Congress into a special session at the earliest possible moment so that it could legitimatize bank closings and could consider emergency legislation in order for solvent banks to reopen and conduct business.

A week later, on Sunday, March 12th, President Roosevelt gave his initial fireside chat. On this precedent-setting occasion, he discussed legislation for control of federal reserve banks, and he dramatically ordered a bank holiday to stop the run on banks. His talk on the complicated subject of banking was worded so simply that it led humorist Will Rogers to observe, "He made everybody understand it, even the bankers!" Herbert Hoover in his presidency had proposed a similar idea but had used the word "moratorium" rather than "holiday." Hoover's word choice sounded funereal and frightened more people than did the word "holiday" or the manner in which President Roosevelt explained it.

The adaptations to radio talking that Roosevelt had made were clearly evident in this first fireside chat. He and his advisers believed that attention spans of listeners sitting at home could not be held for any long period of time; consequently, all the fireside chats as they were soon called were short, none lasting more than thirty minutes. The first one was much briefer, taking only fourteen minutes.

Sunday evenings at 10:00 P.M. Eastern Standard Time was the preferred schedule. Some writers put the number of such broadcasts at twenty-one, other claimed as many as thirty-one. Discrepancies arose because neither Steve Early, Roosevelt's press secretary, nor Roosevelt himself officially classified the talks. The name "fireside chat" was given by a radio reporter who lifted the phrase from a remark Steven Early had given him: "The President likes to think of his audience as being a few people around his fireside."[5]

President Roosevelt considered the recommendation from Moley and Woodin in regard to calling a special session of Congress and talked the idea over with one or two other consultants before endorsing it. On March 5th, he made his move and summoned the 73rd Congress to convene in special session four days later.

In 1932, when thirteen million American men and women could find no work, banks collapsed by the score, robbing depositors of dollars they had earned and thought they were saving. Bustling factories, which a few years earlier had striven to fill orders, now laid off their workers, locked gates, and closed—some forever. In cities, soup kitchens and bread lines kept some of the unemployed alive, but just barely. Wretched shantytowns grew like weeds on the margins of once prosperous urban districts. Across the country, parents and children were going to bed hungry, and no one understood how it could happen in such a rich, formerly thriving nation.

Understandingly, banking and financial institutions were highest on the incoming President's agenda. The first New Deal measure—the Emergency Banking Act—provided for the reopening of banks, and was passed by Congress in the record time of less than eight hours.

Idealistic Franklin Roosevelt in 1933 brought with him into the White House ideas more vague than specific, but almost immediately from the fertile minds of his "Brain Trust" came prodding for active programs. From the helter-skelter around him, a central idea soon began taking shape: the New Deal was going to be built around *industrial planning* [emphasis supplied].

At the end of June 1933, President Roosevelt took a few days off to cruise the New England coast, returning to Washington, D.C. on Independence Day to find two of his chief lieutenants striving for opposite goals. Budget Director Lewis Douglas, noted for passion in restraining expenses, had not wanted public works funded by the federal government to be linked with the NRA. Nor did he think it wise to put implementation of such programs on the chief executive.

By the time FDR was inaugurated for his first administration, most citizens had lost faith in banks and were putting their small funds in postal savings, which had grown from one-hundred-fifty million in 1928 to one billion. There had been runs on banks in Chicago and Detroit, with armored trucks hauling cash out to branch institutions, and on March 4, 1933, Inauguration Day, one newspaper declared, "Thirty States Now on Bank Holidays."

In its special session—from March 9 until June 16, 1933—the 73rd Congress passed social and economic measures, including ones to regulate banks, distribute funds to the unemployed, create jobs, raise agricultural prices, and set wage and production standards for industry.

CHAPTER 13: EARLY NEW DEAL

A period of machine-gun legislation historians label the "Hundred Days" began immediately. Congress was in a mood to do the entire bidding of the leader who had promised a New Deal. FDR interpreted his election as a mandate for action, and when he sent over proposed legislation, Congress, where Democrats had won overwhelming majorities, rubber-stamped it. In the House of Representatives, 435 members were impressionable freshmen congressmen, washed in on the Democratic tide.

In the first two years of the 1930s, the crisis in Western Europe had caused European gold to be withdrawn from American banks. England and most of the nations of the world went off the gold standard, a move that immediately devalued their own currencies. European holdings of American securities were dumped on the market, and American trade with those nations declined disastrously.

In early February, 1932, before Franklin Roosevelt had been sworn in, President Hoover had proposed to Congress creation of a government-lending agency with authority to issue tax-exempt bonds and with wide powers to extend credit. His proposal resulted in establishment of the Reconstruction Finance Corporation, authorized to borrow to the extent of 2 billion to offer emergency financing for banking institutions. By 1933, the RFC had 1.5 billion out in loans, mostly to banks and railroads. Hoover's measure set a one-year moratorium on reparations and war-debt payments, but the legislation came too late to be truly effective. Nevertheless, the RFC would remain the key finance agency of the incoming New Deal.

On March 6, 1933—two days after he entered office—President Franklin D. Roosevelt took a drastic step. The banking crisis was at its worst, and to meet it he issued a proclamation closing all banking institutions and stopping transactions or exports in gold for four days until Congress could meet in a special session. He called it a "banking holiday." Roosevelt's action halted the flow of gold from the Treasury, and in effect, took the country off the gold standard although it did not do so officially until Congress passed an Act approving the measures on April 19th, a month later.[1]

There had been runs on banks in Chicago and Detroit, with armored trucks hauling cash out to branch institutions, and on March 4, 1933, Inauguration Day, one newspaper declared, "Thirty States Now on Bank Holidays."

Advent of the New Deal brought a flurry of changes. During its first Hundred Days in 1933, there were more than a dozen legislative or executive landmarks. The first New Deal measure—the Emergency Banking Act—provided for the re-opening of banks and was passed by Congress in the record time of less than eight hours. No New Deal measure was more consequential or controversial than the National Industrial Recovery Act (later called the National Recovery Act or more simply the NRA) passed in June. Title I of this far-reaching new law prescribed "codes" for nearly every industry with objectives of reform, collective bargaining, setting maximum hours, minimum wages, and working conditions for all and paid special attention to working conditions for children. Under the impetus of the NRA, organized labor recovered many of the losses it sustained in the half-dozen years immediately following 1929.

In June 1938, Congress dampened further Labor disturbances by passing the Fair Labor Standards Act, providing for an eventual maximum work week of forty hours and a minimum wage of forty cents an hour. More than thirteen million workers were affected, so in effect, most of Labor's demands had been met. The Act's constitutionality was challenged later but sustained by a unanimous decision of the U. S. Supreme Court.[2]

At the end of June 1933, President Roosevelt took a few days off to cruise the New England coast, returning to Washington, D.C. on Independence Day to find two of his chief lieutenants striving for opposite goals. Budget Director Lewis Douglas, noted for passion in restraining expenses, had not wanted public works funded by the federal government to be linked with the NRA. Nor did he think it wise to put implementation of such programs on the chief executive.

On the other side, Rexford Guy Tugwell, an early member of the Brain Trust, a former Columbia University economics professor, and now assistant to Henry Wallace, the new Secretary of Agriculture, scoffed at the cost-cutting goals ex-pressed by Budget Director Douglas. Advisor Tugwell put little faith in the scat-tered signs of economic recovery. True, the index of industrial production had risen since Inauguration Day—it had stood at 56 in March and now in July had reached 101. The New York Stock Exchange reported that the monthly volume of shares traded increased six-fold in the same period, from 20 million in February to 125 million in June.[3]

In its special session—from March 9 until June 16, 1933—the 73rd Congress passed social and economic measures, including ones to regulate banks, distribute funds to the unemployed, create jobs, raise agricultural prices, and set wage and production standards for industry.

Ranks of the unemployed were skyrocketing. The Department of Labor esti-mated that at the beginning of 1931 more than four and a half million workers were idle. Bread lines lengthened and soup kitchens bulged as hungry citizens lined up for a few morsels. From urban centers thousands of jobless families moved to farms or villages where they were surviving on semi-subsistence levels. With relief rolls reaching eighteen million men, women, and children, urban police chiefs worried about possible violence.

During the epochal "Hundred Days" of President Franklin Roosevelt's first administration, he made ten speeches, sent fifteen messages to Congress, talked to the press twice a week, conferred personally or by telephone with foreign statesmen, and made innumerable decisions. Some of the important measures passed during those hectic months include:

March 9, 1933	Emergency Banking Act
March 20, 1933	Economy Act
March 31, 1933	Civilian Conservation Corps
April 19, 1933	Gold Standard Abandoned (ratified in June)
May 12, 1933	Federal Emergency Relief
	Agricultural Adjustment Act
	Emergency Farm Mortgage Act
May 18, 1933	Tennessee Valley Authority Act
May 27, 1933	Truth-in-Securities Act
June 13, 1933	Home Owner's Loan Act
June 16, 1933	National Industrial Recovery Act
June 16, 1933	Glass-Steagall Banking Act

The primary purpose of the Emergency Banking Act was to check immediately the money panic engulfing the nation. Introduced, passed, and approved by Congress all on the same day, March 9th, the Act confirmed all the money measures taken by FDR and his Secretary of the Treasury since Inauguration Day. Congressional votes tell the story: the House vote was unanimous, and the Senate vote was seventy-three to seven.

The resultant law, affecting all national banks and Federal Reserve Banks, gave the President broad discretionary powers over transactions in credit, currency, gold, and silver, including foreign exchange. Gold hoarding and export of it were forbidden and a maximum penalty of ten-thousand dollar fine along with ten years in prison was provided.

Solvent banks in the Federal Reserve System were permitted to open only after being given license by the Treasury Department. The Act also gave the Comptroller of the Currency authority to appoint conservators to care for the assets of insolvent national banks; authorized the Secretary of the Treasury to call in all gold and gold certificates in the country; enlarged the open-market operations of Federal Reserve banks, and empowered the RFC to subscribe to the preferred stock of national banks and trust companies.

The peril of bank panic was abruptly erased and the incidence of bank failures dramatically reduced. The Emergency Banking Act did so well that it would be marked in history as the most unqualified success of all New Deal legislation, if measured in terms of its specific purpose.[4]

A week later, acting on President Roosevelt's request, Congress passed the Economy Act—a law meant to balance the budget of normal expenditures through: 1) reductions of up to 15 percent in salaries of government employees, 2) cuts in veterans' pensions and other allowances, particularly pension payments based on non-service connected disabilities, and 3) reorganization of government agencies with a view toward economy. FDR declared that cost-cuttings brought about under this Act would total at least $500 million annually. Although the measure did result in lessening expenditures, the actual amount saved was about $243 million.[5]

Another piece of legislation during the Hundred Days was the Civilian Conservation Corps—an idea that held special appeal for President Roosevelt. Ridicule and stinging criticisms arose when he first proposed it in general terms; nevertheless, he was determined to see it through, for as his wife Eleanor reminded him almost daily, he had to do something about unemployment relief. He came up with thoughts of creating "a civilian conservation corps to be used in simple work, not interfering with normal employment, and confining itself to forestry, prevention of soil erosion, flood control, and similar projects." Calling in lieutenants from the Congress, he explained his proposal and said, "I estimate that 250,000 men can be given temporary employment by early summer if you give me authority to proceed within the next two weeks."

With the new law on his desk awaiting his signature, wily Franklin Roosevelt acted to disarm critics. He promptly named Robert Fechner the Director of Emergency Conservation Work. Fechner was a thorough AFL man, having been vice-president of the machinists' union, and his appointment did much to smooth Green's ruffled feathers.

Provisions of the CCC Act authorized employment of as many as 250,000 jobless males between the ages of 18 to 25 in reforestation, road construction, prevention of soil erosion, and national park and flood control projects. Work camps were set up for enrollees, each of whom received $30 per month, a portion of which was sent to dependents if needed. Before its demise the CCC had as many as 500,000 men on its rolls, and by the end of 1941 had employed more than 2 million youths.[6]

In the early years of the twentieth century the small liberal arts college in Grinnell, Iowa, had established its reputation for scholarship, and it was to this school that Anna Pickett Hopkins sent her twenty-two-year-old son Harry. During his years at Grinnell, Harry Hopkins apparently neither added scholarship luster nor tarnished it, but he graduated and went east to take his first full-time job as a counselor at a camp for poor children in Bound Brook, New Jersey. In 1913-1914, preceding the outbreak of the First World War, Hopkins' boss asked him to make a study of unemployment in several of the big cities in the East. Hopkins found numbers and conditions that became guiding stars for the rest of his life.

After WWI had ended, Harry Hopkins bounced around in several jobs—all of which were in some way connected with social work. Hopkins had been thrilled to hear by radio Roosevelt's "Happy Warrior" speech nominating Al Smith in 1924, and he first met Franklin Roosevelt during the campaign months of 1928. A seminal act created by Roosevelt when he became Governor of New York was called the Temporary Emergency Relief Administration, and he chose Harry Hopkins to be its director.

In the presidency, Roosevelt, building on the RFC still existing from Hoover years, engineered another law to help the jobless. Passed by the 73rd Congress on

May 12, 1933, the Federal Emergency Relief Act authorized an appropriation of $500 million, allotting half this amount as direct relief to the states and the balance for distribution on the basis of $1 of federal aid for every $3 of state or local funds spent for relief. FDR called on his expediter from New York to be director of the new agency.

Thus Harry Hopkins was catapulted into a position of world importance. For twelve years he would work at a salary lower than the one given him in 1932. He died broke in 1946, but in his years with Roosevelt's federal administrations he had been empowered to spend more than nine billion dollars for relief of others and to direct the expenditure of billions more dollars in the Lend Lease program.[7]

Idealistic Franklin Roosevelt in 1933 brought with him into the White House ideas more vague than specific, but almost immediately from the fertile minds of his Brain Trust came prodding for active programs. From the helter-skelter around him a central idea soon began taking shape: the New Deal was going to be built around *industrial planning* [emphasis supplied].

John Maynard Keynes, a British economist, was a dominant theorist throughout most of the first half of the twentieth century. *Time* magazine judged that his writings, and in particular one of his books, *The General Theory of Employment, Interest, and Money*, "had more influence in a shorter time than other book ever written on economics, including Smith's *The Wealth of Nations* and Marx's *Das Kapital*."[8] Though he favored a planned economy and wide control of economic life by democratic public service corporations, Keynes never wavered from his faith in the capitalistic system.

Keynes already had gained considerable reputation by the year FDR ascended to the U.S. presidency, and in the autumn of 1933, Keynes wrote an open letter to President Roosevelt, sending it first to Felix Frankfurter then at Oxford. The letter was an eloquent expression of Keynes' theories, taking issue with established ideas such as Adam Smith's "invisible hand." Smith argued, for example, that if wages rose too fast, employers would lay off so many workers that wages would fall until they reached the point that employers would start rehiring.

Keynes argued that if during depressions employers sliced wages and laid off workers, then incomes, demands, and production would fall even more. Almost all of the classical economists formerly had contended that during depressions the government should raise taxes and cut spending in order to balance the budget. On the contrary, Keynes insisted that the way out of depression was for the government to cut taxes, reduce interest rates, and spend heavily—deficits be damned.

In his open letter, Keynes noted that President Roosevelt seemed to have a conflict of purpose between economic recovery and reform. Too much emphasis on reform, Keynes suggested, might upset business confidence.

In May 1934, Keynes came to America to receive an honorary degree from Columbia University and during this visit also was able to meet President Roosevelt face to face. Arthur Krock of the *New York Times* chided fellow journalists for failing to recognize the importance of this meeting, and indeed both participants in it had high expectations of what might be gained. In truth though, the get-together was not that significant. Krock had intimated that Keynes' meeting with Roosevelt would have great consequences of increased government spending in order to stimulate business, pump-priming as it was called, but their get-together produced little that was new. Whatever influence Keynes had on President Roosevelt came indirectly from the economist's writings channeled to FDR through advisers such as Frankfurter and Secretary of the Treasury Henry Morgenthau.[9]

FDR and planners around him realized that something had to be done to help farmers weather the economic turmoil sweeping the nation. High on the agenda of the crowded "Hundred Days," therefore, was the Agricultural Adjustment Act.

On the assumption that the Depression was largely traceable to domestic causes, Roosevelt's Brain Trusters came up with internal programs, rather than adopting measures to raise prices on the international markets.

Favoring international trade agreements and drastic tariff cuts was Secretary of State Cordell Hull; opposed to such views were those who advocated internal reform measures. One of the latter group was Secretary of Agriculture Henry Agard Wallace. As editor of *Iowa Homestead and Wallace's Farmer,* Henry Wallace had been won over to arguments for raising farm prices by crop allotments. Wallace thereafter led the President's inner circle in arguing for an "equality for agriculture" program—later known as "parity."

Having won FDR's confidence and secured his endorsement, Wallace and other New Dealers promoted legislation designed to boost farm prices in part by reducing production and by giving birth to programs that paid farmers to leave some acres unattended. There was vigorous debate in Congress where some legislators feared the proposed measures would become permanent, thereby eliminating the fierce independence of American agriculture. Such arguments were overcome though as economic and social fabrics deteriorated further.

Foreclosures on farm properties multiplied, and so-called "dollar auctions" became a regular occurrence in states like Iowa. When a farmer's property was to be foreclosed, banks would schedule a public auction. Neighbors would arrive at the auction site, carrying shotguns to ensure the original owner could buy back the land at $1 or less.

During the second week of March, 1933, President Roosevelt sent to Congress his farm relief message for reduction of acreage in certain basic crops and for credit relief to farmers who were faced with losing their homes. The resulting Agricultural Adjustment Act, passed two months later, declared as its objective the establishment of farm prices at a level "that will give agricultural commodities a purchasing power with respect to articles farmers buy, equivalent to the purchasing power of agricultural commodities in the base period . . ." i. e. August 1909 to July 1914, a period arbitrarily adopted as a time when agricultural prices had approached equality to industrial ones.

Beginning with the basic staples—wheat, cotton, corn, hogs, rice, milk, and tobacco—the list of restricted crops expanded steadily as the government provided attractive benefit payments or commodity loans to cooperating farmers. An army of agents from the Department of Agriculture roamed America to persuade farmers to plow under or otherwise reduce their crop production. Throughout the Midwest, there was wholesale slaughtering of pigs, and in the South cotton growers plowed under or eliminated more than ten and a half million acres out of a total of forty million. The farmers' cash income rose from $4.5 billion in 1932 to $6.9 billion in 1935.[10]

Chief object of the Agricultural Adjustment Act (Triple A) law was to curtail overproduction and establish "parity" prices for some of the most important commodities. Parity price was based on the purchasing power of the farmer's dollar at the level of 100 cents during the period between 1906 for corn, cotton, wheat, rice, hogs, and dairy products; the base period for tobacco was taken from the period 1919-1929. In return for voluntarily reducing crops or acreage, farmers were granted direct benefits or rental payments. The Act established a new agency— the Agricultural Adjustment Administration, immediately called the Triple A.

The Triple A relieved the credit crisis for countless farmers by providing refinancing of mortgages through the agency of the Federal Land Banks. In addition, an amendment to the Act permitted the President to inflate the currency by the following means: devaluation of the gold content of the dollar, free coinage of silver at a ratio to gold determined by the President, and issuance of paper currency to the amount of $3 billion. This last named provision was never implemented by FDR, but the Triple A enabled him to raise prices through control of the so-called "commodity dollar."

CHAPTER 14: FDR'S SECOND ADMINISTRATION

By the time FDR began active campaigning for a second term, America was showing signs of economic progress. Perhaps the black horse of poverty had run its course. Whatever the reason, citizens were climbing out of the deepest holes of the Depression. Unemployment had dropped by about four million; payrolls in manufacturing industries had doubled; stock prices had done even better; total cash income of farmers had risen by $3 billion; commercial and industrial failures were a third of what they had been four years earlier, and industrial production had doubled. Roosevelt and his coterie attributed it all to the New Deal.

Indeed, some of the measures indisputably had helped. The Tennessee Valley Authority was an example.

During the First World War, the government had built a large hydroelectric power plant and two munitions factories at Muscle Shoals on the Tennessee River in the northwest corner of Alabama. For fifteen years afterward, various administrations had tried unsuccessfully to dispose of the Muscle Shoals facilities to private interests.

A month after moving into the White House, FDR wrote a letter to Senator George Norris, Republican from Nebraska, a leader in movements toward federal water power regulation and for public ownership and operation of hydroelectric plants. The President's letter expressed the hope to get a bill through Congress "which would allow us to spend $25 million this year to put 25,000 families on farms at an average cost of $1,000 per family. It can be done.... Will you talk this over with some of your fellow dreamers on the Hill?"[1]

With guidance from Norris and others in Congress, Roosevelt got his $25 million; it was intended to resettle families into a planned community named Arthurdale, ten miles southeast of Morgantown, West Virginia. The Arthurdale experiment became prototype for the much more gigantic federal project—the Tennessee Valley Authority.

Senator Norris, a liberal progressive who linked the 1890s with the 1930s, was no great orator and was physically unimpressive—he never acquired a dinner coat during thirty years in Washington. The Senator talked often of "one great central problem, the use of the earth for the good of man." Having grown up during hard times in Nebraska near the close of the nineteenth century, Norris never yielded on his dream of making the Republican Party an instrument of human progress and justice. TVA gave him an outlet for such unbounded energy.

The Tennessee River is formed by the confluence of other rivers arising in North Carolina and southwestern Virginia. Fed also by smaller streams on the west slope of the Appalachians, the Tennessee flows southwestward past Knoxville, Chattanooga, and Chickamauga into northern Alabama. Passing over the Muscle Shoals, it has dropped 137 feet in slightly less than 37 miles. In the years before 1933, a river 652 miles long and one of the greatest in the country could be turned into a valley with heavier rainfall than any other region except the Pacific Northwest and subjected to disastrous floods, denuding the land with devastating effects upon families trying to scratch out a living.

In January 1933, even before taking office, FDR visited Muscle Shoals and began envisioning changing the region through use and control of its water resources. With Norris and other Congressional leaders interested in water and power controls, he began pushing for legislation which would advance the social and economic welfare of the entire Tennessee region, much like the experiment at Arthurdale in West Virginia had done.

Land in the proposed Tennessee region was indeed impoverished. It had been stripped of timber after the Civil War, and now more than a million families in the barren land lived on a diet of cornmeal and salt pork. One could go to towns like Savannah, Tennessee, or Decatur, Alabama, and see ragged children, undernourished and staring vacant-eyed. Land sold for the taxes owed, and a third of the population had malaria, tuberculosis, pellagra, or trachoma. Half the valley's people lived on farms, and 97 percent of those farms had no electricity.

In the euphoria of the Hundred Days, Congress was quick to create the Tennessee Valley Authority, although many did not know exactly what it was. They were told by Norris and fellow proponents that the Muscle Shoals project involved flood control, land reclamation, prevention of soil erosion, afforestation, the elimination of marginal lands from cultivation, and the distribution and diversification of industry.

The TVA Act set up an independent public corporation with a board of three directors and was authorized to construct dams and power plants throughout a region encompassing parts of Tennessee, North Carolina, Kentucky, Virginia, Mississippi, Georgia, and Alabama. When asked by reporters what TVA was supposed to be, FDR replied that it wasn't just for navigation and control; it was a *regional* agency for reclaiming land and human beings. Not all critics were satisfied. The *New York Times* called the project "Congressional folly," and one representative in the House said it was "patterned closely after one of the Soviet dreams."[2] Supporters rebutted that the Act not only would build dams to control floods and generate cheap power, but the rates it set would become a yardstick for private power companies.

The TVA brought to the land of Daniel Boone—a land of exhausted soils, eroded hills, sharecroppers, and prevailing malnutrition—new hopes and vitality.

Before the gigantic plan was enacted, the standard of living was compared unfavorably with that of peasants in Eastern Europe. Floods often swept away houses, livestock, and other property. Industrialists had cut down valuable hardwood forests and destroyed vegetation by exuding ugly chemical wastes, and, of course, electrical power in the region was too expensive for all but a chosen few.

After TVA got into full swing, inexpensive phosphate fertilizers from the system revived the soil; demonstration farming techniques diversified the crops, and increased production a thousand fold. And most important, TVA supplied electric power at greatly reduced rates to 425,000 householders, many of whom enjoyed benefits of electricity for the first time. David Lilienthal, one of three original directors of TVA, in 1944 would write:

Power has come to the farms of this region, 85,000 of them in seven states, about one in every five. Ten years ago, there was electricity on only one Mississippi farm out of a hundred; in Georgia, one out of thirty-six; in Tennessee and Alabama one in twenty-five . . . There now are refrigerators in kitchens . . . There are hay driers in barns, freezing lockers in crossroads stores. There are community food dehydrators, small motors to grind feed, cut the wood, turn a small lathe. Power is curing hams, processing sweet potatoes, cooling milk in the new dairies.[3]

In the years between TVA's establishment in 1933 and the close of the Second World War, facilities of the "experimental project" would build and operate nine main-river dams as well as numerous subsidiary ones along lesser streams. Moreover, during the forty-four-and-a-half months of that war, TVA supplied the power for manufacturing munitions, aluminum, and the vital atom bomb plant at Oak Ridge, Tennessee. More than a show piece, the Tennessee Valley Authority would remain one of the great triumphs of the New Deal.

Following passage of the TVA Act, FDR persuaded Congressional cohorts with their dominance to enact other legislation aimed toward relieving the stricken citizenry. At the end of May came the Federal Securities Act, a law designed to compel full disclosure to investors of information relating to new securities publicly offered, sold through the mails, or in interstate commerce. There were certain exceptions, but nearly all new issues had to be registered with the Federal Trade Commission together with sworn statements placed on public file. A year later, this function was transferred to the Securities and Exchange Commission.

In the year Franklin Roosevelt entered the White House, the nation's farmers were drowning in indebtedness, owing more than $12 billion, most of which was in mortgages. Orthodox methods taken by President Hoover had been ineffective, and the new administration struck out boldly by engineering the Home Owners Refinancing Act.

This Act, which passed the Democratic-controlled Congress the second week in June, created the Home Owners Loan Corporation with a capital stock of $200 million drawn from the RFC and an authorized issue of $2 billion in bonds to refinance home mortgage debts for nonfarm owners. Refinancing was accomplished by exchanging HOLC bonds for mortgages and all other financial obligations up to a total of $14,000, which then were converted into a single first mortgage. The

HOLC was also empowered to furnish cash advances for taxes, repair, and maintenance up to 50 percent of appraised value on unencumbered property.

By making credit available to those who wanted to redeem property already foreclosed or to reduce other claims against their holdings, thousands of small homeowners who faced eviction were saved by the HOLC. By 1936, when it ceased operation, the HOLC had made more than a million loans involving well over $3 billion. Unquestionably, it was another agency that played a major role in stemming the collapse of real estate values in the darkest years of the Depression.

Seldom was the prestige of bankers as low as during the spring of 1933. Senate investigating committees exposed shockingly illegal practices in management and manipulation of investments. The public was startled, for instance, to learn that financier J.P. Morgan had used tax loopholes to escape paying taxes in 1930, 1931, and 1933.

Small wonder, therefore, that a banking law, somewhat lesser understood than others initiated by the new administration, was passed within days of enactment of the HOLC. The Banking Act of 1933, more familiarly known as the Glass-Steagall Act, named for Senator Carter Glass from Virginia and Representative Henry B. Steagall of Alabama—the two who nursed it through Congress—was a law that at first guaranteed individual bank deposits under $5,000.

The bill sailed through the House on a vote of 262 to 19, and the Senate passed it by acclamation. In its final form, the Glass-Steagall Act established a Federal Deposit Insurance Corporation (later known as FDIC) which, beginning on January 1, 1934, would totally insure nearly all individual deposits in banks covered, for less than 5 percent of all deposits in America, which at the time were individually more $2,500. On July 1, 1934, when the permanent insurance scheme went into effect, the FDIC would totally insure all deposits up to $10,000, 75 percent of all deposits of $10,000 to $50,000, and 50 percent of all deposits over $50,000.

The Glass-Steagall Act also curbed the dangers of stock market speculation by compelling commercial banks to divest themselves of investment affiliates—a provision aimed at banks which had conducted highly speculative and illegal operations under cover of an affiliated corporation with results that were ruinous to depositors and often to the bank itself.

It had been an extremely productive session of the U.S. Congress in that spring of 1933, but before it closed, there was another bit of legislation—a law which later generations would mark as the single most lasting Act of the New Deal.

CHAPTER 15: SECURITY FOR THE AGED

As in most large political or economic advances, security for the elderly did not spring suddenly from an individual brainstorm.

For the first seventeen hundred years of the Christian Era, care, if any, for the aged or the infirm was seen as a local responsibility. During the Middle Ages, merchants and craftsmen—individuals who had a common trade or business—started banding together to form mutual aid societies. These groups regulated production and employment as well as sometimes providing a range of benefits to their members, including financial help in times of poverty or illness. A few of the scattered aid groups offered contributions to help defray expenses when a member died but, as might be expected, such care was minimal and haphazard.

Until the opening of the seventeenth century, throughout the European countries relief for the poor or indigent was considered a local responsibility. Individuals who had a common trade or business banded together to form mutual aid groups which regulated employment and provided a range of benefits to members, including financial help in times of poverty or illness as well as contributions to help defray expenses when a member died.

England in 1601 adopted a set of "Poor Laws" which relied on taxation to support the destitute. The English "Poor Laws" discriminated between the "worthy" and "unworthy" poor and represent a systematic enactment to accept responsibility of the state to provide for the welfare of its citizens. These Poor Laws represent the first systematic legislation in democratic governments to provide for the welfare of its citizens, and it was this tradition that pilgrims brought with them when they journeyed to the New World.

In colonial America, Poor Laws depended upon local taxation, and, as in the English prototype, the distribution of such funds discriminated between the "worthy" and the "unworthy" poor. It was up to town elders to decide who was worthy. As villages and towns grew larger and more complex, local taxation for relief was severely strained. Nevertheless, throughout the eighteenth and nineteenth centuries most states, as well as many counties, had established houses for the poor. The role of government, though, was kept to minimum. Even as late as 1915, at most only 25 percent of monies spent on relief for the poor came from public funds. Taxpayers wanted to "discourage" dependency, so living conditions in "poor houses" were grim and restrictive. Those receiving such relief lost their personal property, the right to vote, the right to move, and in some cases were required to wear a large "P" on their clothing.

The year of 1920 marked a turning point, for that was the first year in U. S. history when more citizens in its country were living in cities than on farms. Americans were moving from farms and small communities to large cities—where industrial jobs were. In 1890, for example, only 28 percent of the population lived in cities; by 1930, this percentage had exactly doubled to 56 percent.

The decade of the 1930s found America facing its worst economic crisis. Twenty-five percent of the work force had no jobs; hobos wandered aimlessly around the country, banks and businesses failed, and a majority of elderly citizens lived in dependency. Huey Long's *Share the Wealth* plan flourished briefly but died with its founder. Dr. Townsend's pension scheme calling for a federal payment of $200 per month for every citizen sixty years of age or older was derided by most recognized economists. Out of America's fascination with technology had come another eccentric reform movement known as Technocracy. This sect had been founded shortly after WWI and argued that the nation's only hope was to let engineers and other technology experts run the country on engineering principles. The rallying cry was "production for use" rather than production for profit in the capitalist system. Other abortive plans for relief of the elderly were pushed by scattered adherents, but those panaceas, too, were dumped into the dustbin of history by a monumental act generated by New Deal Brain Trusters. Circumstances demanded change.

Several of Franklin Roosevelt's advisors would later garner credit for spurring the Social Security Act of 1935, but there can be no dispute that Secretary of Labor Frances Perkins was one of the Act's most fervent proponents. Before joining the New Deal Administration in Washington, Perkins had held various positions in New York State governments. In 1918 she accepted Governor Al Smith's offer to become the first female member of that state's Industrial Commission, becoming chairwoman of the group in 1926.

Al Smith was a practical politician from the old school, and at his funeral in 1944, two of his cronies were overheard in their speculations on why he had turned social reformer. One of them summed up the matter: "*I'll tell you why. Smith read a book. That book was a person, and her name was Frances Perkins. She told him all these things, and he believed her.*"[1]

In 1929 newly-elected New York Governor Franklin Roosevelt re-appointed Perkins as the State Industrial Commissioner, and in that position she helped put the Empire State in the forefront of progressive reform. Perkins brought about expanded factory investigations, reduced the work week for women to 48 hours, and championed minimum wage and unemployment laws.

Three years later, one of Franklin Roosevelt's earliest appointments as president in the White House came when he chose Frances Perkins to be Secretary of Labor. She was the first woman to hold a cabinet position in the U.S. and at that time to be in the presidential line of succession. Perkins and Secretary of the Interior Harold Ickes were the only cabinet members to retain their posts throughout the years of FDR's presidencies.

Perkins wrote most of the New Deal legislation dealing with minimum-wage laws, but undeniably her most important contribution was serving as chairwoman of the President's Committee on Economic Security. In this post, she was a key player in all aspects of the origin, reports, and hearings that ultimately resulted in the Social Security Act of 1935.

The Social Security Act as Congress first enacted it did not provide universal coverage for retirement benefits; instead, the Act established benefits principally for industrial employees. Employment definitions reflected typical white male categories and patterns; excluded were many workers, farm laborers, the self-employed, household servants, casual laborers, and the unemployed.

The new law set up a federal pension system funded by taxes on employers and employees. Contrary to older legislation, this new plan was not "needs based;" rather, its theory was that workers still employed would contribute to those already retired. Employed workers would in turn receive benefits upon their own retirement funded by taxes paid by others still working and from new workers entering the marketplace. Originally, Social Security contributions were equal to a tax of three percent on salaries up to $3,000; both employee and employer paid the tax into the Social Security fund. Later laws increased the percentage of contributions to 6.2 percent from employee and employers, making a total of 12.4 percent on salaries up to $76,200.[2]

From its outset the Social Security Act was controversial. Critics claimed the legislation would cause a loss of jobs, but proponents rebutted that it would encourage older workers to retire, thereby creating opportunities for younger people to find jobs, which in turn would lower the still staggering unemployment rate.

By 1936, various aspects of New Deal legislation were on the docket of the U.S. Supreme Court, and among them was the Social Security Act. The Court, in a five to four decision, upheld the constitutionality of the Act in a case marked *Steward Machine Company v. Davis*, 301 U.S. 548, (1937).[3] Justices in the minority opined that the act went beyond powers granted to the federal government in the Constitution. They argued that by imposing a tax on employers that could be avoided only by contributing to a state unemployment-compensation fund, the federal government essentially was forcing the state to establish an unemployment-compensation fund that would meet its criteria. The federal government had no power to enact such a program.

The majority view, however, was: "It is too late today for the argument to be heard with tolerance that in a crisis so extreme the use of the moneys of the nation to relieve the unemployed and their dependents is a use for any purpose narrower than the promotion of the general welfare."[4]

Rulings issued from the Court on the same day in a second case involving the Social Security Act's validity, 301 U.S. 619 (1937), the program was further upheld. In this suit the Court judged: "The proceeds of both [employee and employer] taxes are to be paid into the Treasury like internal-revenue taxes generally, and are not earmarked in any way." Thus, social security taxes were constitutional as a mere exercise of Congress's general taxation powers.[5]

The practical effects of these two cases affirmed the Social Security Act's constitutionality, but another pivotal bit of New Deal legislation—the National Industrial Recovery Act—was yet to be decided.

Chapter 16: Supreme Court Imbroglio

Passage of the Banking Act helped shore up financial institutions, and the Triple A was in place to revitalize the nation's distressed farmers. One more measure was needed—a shotgun law which would stimulate industrial and business activity, thereby reducing unemployment. With those goals in mind, a bill prepared by Democratic stalwarts drew little debate and was passed hurriedly by the 73rd Congress on the day it adjourned, June 16, 1933.

Named the National Industrial Recovery Act, later shortened simply to the NRA, the program would become one of the New Deal's most touted and yet most controversial enactments. The act aimed to revive industrial and business activity and to reduce unemployment—the most visible sores of the Depression. Actions under codes and agreements were exempt from operations of antitrust laws, and courts could issue injunctions against violators. A high-minded idea, the NRA was based on the principle of industrial self-regulation, operating under government supervision through a system of fair competition codes. Fair trade codes had been set up and used by industrial and related associations in the period following the First World War. With the New Deal in full flow, the NRA was begun with new, fair competition codes to be approved by the President and enforceable by law. The President was given authority to prescribe the codes and to make agreements or approve voluntary agreements.

One section of the NRA Act, Section 7a, guaranteed labor's right "to organize and bargain collectively through representatives of their own choosing." Title II of the Act established the Public Works Administration (WPA). FDR put crusty Secretary of the Interior Harold I. Ickes in charge of the WPA, which during its lifetime and under his aegis spent a total of $4,250 million on more than 34,000 public projects.[1]

The President first picked General Hugh S. Johnson to head the NRA. Johnson had graduated from West Point in 1903 and had helped draft the Selective Service Act used during World War I. At the end of that conflict, he had left army service and had campaigned vigorously for FDR in the '32 election.

At the outset of the NRA, Johnson was highly recognized for his prior achievements and was chosen by *Time* magazine as its 1933 "Man of the Year." "Old Iron Pants," as he was called, threw his evangelistic style into promoting the NRA, and its symbol, the "blue eagle," flew in store windows and business establishments across the nation.

Almost immediately, the colorful, outspoken, and opinionated Johnson began to rankle business leaders. They complained he was dictatorial, and it was not long before he was criticized for having fascist tendencies. By1934 his reputation had lost lots of its luster.

FDR's naming of Ickes to lead the WPA put Hugh Johnson in a subservient role. Humiliated and angered, Johnson's language grew more intemperate as he came under attacks by officials within the Administration and increasing volleys from the public. Some historians ascribe his fall to inherent contradictions in the NRA; others attribute it to his acknowledged drinking. Whatever the cause, he was faltering badly by 1934, and FDR replaced him. Although Johnson's enthusiasm had lost most of its vigor when the '36 election rolled around, he still supported FDR.

Eight months after the seminal NRA had been passed by Congress, a National Recovery Board, primarily to enforce labor's right to collective bargaining, was established. Three months later, this body submitted a gloomy report, alleging that, to the detriment of small businesses, the parent NRA agency was encouraging monopoly and cartelization.

Charged with enforcement of collective bargaining practices, the NLRB could ban company unions as well as employers for interferences with union organizing. The Board was given authority to investigate an employee's charge of unfair labor practices (such as intimidation, espionage, discrimination, etc.), and could summon the employer for a trial hearing. If the charges were upheld by the NLRB, it could issue a "cease and desist" order enforceable by federal courts.

Business and financial leaders saw such measures as intrusions upon their basic rights. Adverse reactions to the NRA mounted, and even some old guard New Dealers broke ranks. Then a legal case, the formal name of which was *Schechter Poultry Corporation vs. United States*, set off nationwide repercussions as it percolated its way to the Supreme Court.

The challenge had originated when the Schechter brothers, operators of a Brooklyn poultry business, were convicted of violating the NRA's Live Poultry Code by selling diseased chickens and by disregarding the code's wage-and-hour provisions. When appeals reached the Supreme Court, attorneys for the Administration insisted that the grave economic emergency had made codes and empowerment of the President necessary. The Court brushed aside such arguments and, in May 1935, passed a unanimous decision ruling that in approving the National Industrial Recovery Act, Congress had exceeded its authority. "Extraordinary conditions do not create or enlarge constitutional powers," ruled the nation's highest tribunal.[2]

During his first press conference following that judicial decision, an embittered President Roosevelt asserted that the Court's action had rendered the powers of the federal government to "the horse and buggy age." There already was enough controversy, but FDR's statement denigrating the Court's judgment made the bubbling stew rise higher.

FDR's opponents fought back in Congress, in newspapers and magazines, and over air waves. On one Sunday evening during prime time listening hours, a leading businessman used the Columbia Broadcasting System to retaliate to FDR's "horse and buggy age" metaphor.

The speaker admitted that throughout history there indeed had been great changes. Society had moved from cartwheel, to stagecoach, to saddlebags, pony express, telegraph, steamboats, railways, automobiles, and even to airplanes. Families now owned automobiles, and parking lots at Detroit were filled to overflowing. However, individual men and women had made the achievements and had done so without government shackles such as the NRA. "If you want something done, you must do it yourself." If one man can do it, others can and will. It was the man in the driver's seat who brought progress to society. "Free enterprise," the speaker insisted, "is the spinal cord of progress."[3]

Former President Herbert Hoover, Senators Hiram Johnson, William Borah, Gerald Nye, and other Republican spokesmen jumped into the debate along with scribes from the media. One of the latter, acerbic H. L. Mencken, wrote that in 1932 America had been told utopia was on its way, and he added,

Wizards of the highest amperage . . . were on hand to do the job, and they were armed with new and infallible arcana. . . But what did these wizards turn out to be? Once on the job they were the sorriest mob of mountebanks ever gathered together at one time—even in Washington . . . vapid young pedagogues, out-of-work YMCA secretaries, third-rate journalists, briefless lawyers, and soaring chicken farmers. . . As for the President, he has survived for a long time through the very flexibility of his principles. . . If he became convinced tomorrow that coming out for cannibalism would get him votes . . . he would begin fattening a missionary in the White House backyard come Wednesday. [4]

Conservative critics attracted converts, and in the summer of 1935 Republican prospects began looking up. Roosevelt's popularity sagged in the next winter, and in August of the following year the GOP won a congressional election in Rhode Island. The Republican upsurge continued in November when the party captured the city of Philadelphia and the New York State Assembly.

Herbert Hoover led the old guard in speeches denouncing regimentations of the New Deal, but he offered only past formulas: retrenchment, a balanced budget, the gold standard, the tariff, and return of relief measures to control by the states. In addition to Hoover, other possible Republican candidates for the presidency included Senators William E. Borah from Idaho and Arthur H. Vandenberg of Michigan, and Frank Knox, publisher of the Chicago Daily News.

Then a dark horse, Governor Alfred M. Landon of Kansas, joined the nomination-seeking pack.

Republicans held their convention in Cleveland the second week in June, 1936, and on the first ballot chose the dark horse to lead their ticket. Alfred Landon, the only Republican governor elected in 1932 to survive the Democratic landslide two years later, was an old Bull Mooser more liberal than the party that nominated him. He did not see the New Deal as a plot to undercut American institutions and in fact had supported some New Deal programs.

Landon could boast of a balanced budget in his home state, and it was thought he would win agricultural votes throughout the Midwest. A sincere, plain-speaking man with little magnetism, Landon lacked the style of FDR; journalists called him a "Kansas Coolidge." He had declined to fly to Cleveland to accept the nomination for fear such a gesture would appear to be aping his opponent's dramatic flight to Chicago four years earlier.

For their convention during the last week in June, Democrats met in Philadelphia. The gathering was more coronation than convention, for there was no question FDR would be chosen again. Senator Alben Barkley of Kentucky delivered the keynote address, and in it gave a sonorous defense of the New Deal, addressing also the furor caused by the Supreme Court's decision.

"Over against the hosannas of Hoover for the tortured interpretation of the Constitution of this nation," intoned Barkley to uproarious applause from delegates, "I place the tortured souls and bodies of its working men, women, and children." The trouble lay not with the Constitution , he said, but with the men who interpreted it. The Democratic Party wanted the Court to treat the Constitution "as a life-giving charter, rather than an object of curiosity on the shelf of a museum."[5]

Barkley's language reinforced FDR's convictions, and the election that fall was lackluster. Landon's tours and unpretentious campaigning failed to convince many voters. Democrats garnered nearly twenty-five million votes compared with sixteen million given Republicans. Results from the electoral college were even more overwhelming: for Democrats 98.49 percent, or 523 votes—46 states—all states except Maine and Vermont; and for Republicans, 1.51 percent, or 8 votes— 2 states.[6]

Buoyed by the size of his victory and with his dander up from the rebuke suffered by Supreme Court rulings, Roosevelt vowed to continue the fight. Particularly galling was knowing he was the first American President to serve a four-year term without being able to name a single Supreme Court Justice. To him it was obvious the body was dominated by conservatives who used their own economic and social biases to interpret the Constitution.

He talked the matter over with advisors, some of whom recommended taking the problem to congressional leaders. After all, Congress had the power to reenact laws voided by the Supreme Court and to raise the number of justices required to invalidate a Congressional Act from a simple majority to perhaps six or even seven votes. Other confidants suggested launching arguments for a constitutional amendment, but FDR learned that two thirds of Congress and three quarters of state legislatures were necessary for a constitutional amendment. Opponents could easily choke off that avenue.

Besides, FDR insisted, the trouble lay not in the Constitution itself but in the old men interpreting it. The President asked his attorney general to search files for any precedents, and the search revealed a plan proposed in 1913 under President Woodrow Wilson—an idea for empowering the President of the United States to appoint a new federal judge for every one with ten years of service who had reached the age of seventy and failed to retire. There was nothing sacred about the actual number of justices on the Supreme Court. John Adams had cut the original six members down to five, and Jefferson had upped the membership to seven. Twenty-three years prior to the Civil War, the Court was set at nine, and under Lincoln's administration it had increased to ten. After the Civil War, the Court was decreased to eight members, and in 1869 increased again to nine, its membership in 1936.

FDR pounced on the scheme offered by his attorney general, saying it was "the answer to a maiden's prayer." Spokesmen on the other side, equally fervent, immediately labeled it "court packing." By the end of January 1937, FDR was ready to fire his weapons.

On the thirtieth of that month, while movie stars and other celebrities were assembling downstairs in the White House for his annual Birthday Ball, FDR held a private luncheon upstairs with only four trusted associates. After dishes had been cleared, he read aloud a letter from his attorney general—one of the attendees—recounting workloads and delayed cases on dockets of judicial courts everywhere, including the Supreme Court. Then came his stunning revelation: he was going to submit a proposal dealing with judges in any federal court—including the Supreme Court—who had reached the age of seventy. The plan, in essence, provided that whenever a judge of that age in any federal court refused to avail himself of his existing statutory opportunity to retire on a pension, an additional judge should be appointed to that court by the President with approval of the Senate. There was no discussion by attendees at the luncheon—just FDR's announcement.

A White House Judiciary Dinner was scheduled for February 2, 1937. In accordance with custom, all members of the Supreme Court were invited. Other guests that evening brought the number of attendees to slightly over ninety. Toasts were drunk honoring the Court, and discussion over cocktails was more serious than usual. After the meal, the ladies retired to the Blue Room and the men went into the Green Room, where FDR chatted and joked with seven of the Supreme Court Justices—two members, Justice Louis Brandeis and Justice Harlan Stone, had been unable to attend.

When the party broke up and guests had left, FDR asked Sam Rosenman, by this time his chief speech writer, to stay and work on a message announcing the Court scheme. FDR had called a Cabinet meeting for the next morning and had invited key congressional leaders, including the chairmen of the Senate and House Judiciary Committees, along with Speaker of the House Bankhead, Democratic House Leader Sam Rayburn, and Joe Robinson, the Democratic Senate leader. A press conference where FDR intended to disclose the Court plan would follow the Cabinet gathering.

At the opening of the press conference, President Roosevelt read his prepared message about revising the Supreme Court. There was no discussion or further questioning then, but as soon as the plan became public, explosions began. Opposition came from the Congress, from the Court itself, and from almost the entire press of the nation. Congressional attacks were carried on more violently and bitterly by members of Roosevelt's own party than by the Republicans.

As soon as FDR's plan for reorganizing the judiciary reached Capitol Hill, supporters in both Senate and House dropped it into respective legislative hoppers. Seams in the New Deal coalition that had won victory in the preceding fall's election came apart so quickly that even FDR himself was surprised. Battle lines for the coming fight formed and hardened quickly.

Conservative politicians and newspapers gleefully jumped on the plan, and Former President Hoover warned, "Hands off the Supreme Court!" The public was upset, for it had not been informed through previous planning and coordination. People needed time to consider an attack upon such a venerable institution as the Supreme Court.

The President had struck a tender nerve, sending shock waves everywhere. The stock market dropped; Chambers of Commerce, Daughters of the American Revolution, the Liberty League, American Legion, National Association of Manufacturers, civic clubs, and organizations of all sorts passed denunciatory resolutions. Ordinary voters flooded their elected representatives with pleas to save the country from "dictatorship."

FDR retaliated, and on March 4th, at a hundred-dollar-a-plate dinner celebrating his victory at the polls in the preceding November, he called upon Democrats to close ranks and preserve gains made over the past four years. Lashing out at the Supreme Court, he claimed that by electing him a second time American citizens wanted to throw off shackles of the past. Reform measures, however, were being continually frustrated in New Deal efforts to make the democratic process work. Major programs in response to present needs were being aborted by an antiquated Supreme Court.

A week later he gave a fireside chat in which he offered reasons for his Court proposal. He hoped to quiet public clamor over the plot and to satisfy those who thought a constitutional amendment preferable. In this homey living room setting, FDR said,

It would take months and years thereafter to get a two-thirds majority in favor of that amendment in both Houses of the Congress. Then would come the long course of ratification by three-fourths of all the States . . . Thirteen States which contain only five percent of the voting population can block ratification even though the thirty-five States with ninety-five percent of the population are in favor of it. . .

And remember one thing more. . . An amendment, like the rest of the Constitution, is what the Justices say it is rather than what its framers or you might hope it is.[7]

The U.S. Senate Judiciary Committee opened hearings on the President's proposal the second week in March, and the Administration's case was presented by Homer Cummings, Attorney General, and his assistant Robert Jackson. Questioning of the two was vigorous and buttressed by a team of legal experts from the American Bar Association invited to the hearings by opposition leaders.

Twelve days later, Senator Burton Wheeler began the rebuttal by attacking the nub of the administration's argument: that lethargy from "overaged justices had created a logjam of unresolved cases." Drawing a letter from his pocket, Senator Wheeler dramatically announced, "I have here a letter from the Chief Justice of the Supreme Court, Mr. Charles Evans Hughes, dated March 21, 1937, written by him and approved by Mr. Justice Brandeis and Mr. Justice Van Devanter."

All were astonished! Not within memory had a Chief Justice taken part in a public controversy. Factually and unemotionally, Hughes's seven-page letter refuted the charge that the Court was unable to handle its workload or letting cases stack up. "There is no congestion of cases upon our calendar," he had written, and he supported the contention by showing a statistical table. The addition of more judges, Hughes asserted, would simply mean "more judges to hear, more judges to confer, more judges to discuss, more judges to be convinced and to decide." With consummate skill, the nation's highest judge had wiped out the President's plot to expand the Court.

Arguments by the public and within legislative halls continued, but the battle had been decided by the letter from Chief Justice Hughes. On July 22, 1937, the Supreme Court plan was finally and definitely rejected by the Congress. Roosevelt and New Deal diehards later would insist their arguments had swayed the Court so much that most goals had been achieved anyhow; more dispassionate observers wrote that the President had acted hastily and in anger, making the biggest single mistake thus far in his presidency.

One bit of legislation pushed hard by FDR during the time his proposed revision of the Supreme Court was being debated came with passage of the Rural Electrification Act. Before the start of FDR's second administration, most cities of any size were enjoying benefits of electric power, but the lighted "white way" of a city ended with its limit sign on the outskirt. Farmers had been ignored. Nine out of ten farms in 1933 relied on gas engines, horses, mules, and hand labor for power and on kerosene lamps for light. Nearly twenty-four million of the thirty million citizens then working in agriculture had no bathtub or shower, lived with privies outside, carried water from wells or brooks, heated their homes by stoves, and did laundry and even bathed their children out of doors. Despite repeated appeals from rural folk to private power companies for electric power to light homes and ease workloads, the utilities refused to invest in what they saw as a losing proposition. Without electricity to pump water, heat homes, refrigerate food, wash and iron clothes, milk cows, and light rooms at the pull of a switch, farm families were destined to eke out their lives in primitive fashion.

Eying successes of TVA and with farmers throughout the hinterlands in mind, however, advisors of FDR began urging him to bring electrification to rural areas. Under such goading in 1935, he set up the Rural Electrification Administration as a part of his relief program. This department was meant to function as a lending agency to make long-term, low interest loans to private utility companies so that transmission lines could be built throughout the countryside.

Utility companies balked and replied, "Very few farms now require electricity for major farm operations . . ." In the face of such resistance, congressional proponents led by Senator Norris and allies rallied behind the slogan, "Let's electrify the entire country." In 1936 their efforts resulted in the Rural Electrification Administration being created and made an independent agency with the purpose of giving loans to nonprofit organizations.

Lyndon Baines Johnson, yet to make his marks on the national scene, had been put in charge of the National Youth Administration (NYA) for the State of Texas. The NYA was a New Deal measure aimed at providing employment for youths from relief families and part-time jobs for needy college students. From this position, Johnson began waging a campaign for election to the U. S. House as the Representative from the Tenth Congressional District in Texas—a campaign which led to his first post in Washington, D. C., the following year.

Few sections in America better illustrated the need for electricity than did the Texas Hill Country which Johnson represented. It was the second week of June, 1938, before the young Congressman could get in to see the busy President Roosevelt. Johnson's intent was to ask for the President's support in having the REA bend its rules enough to lend money to central Texas cooperatives so that they could be persuaded to build electricity lines in very sparsely populated areas. In the interview, FDR used his tactics of directing the conversation into irrelevant channels, and soon Johnson's allotted fifteen minutes were up. He never got a chance to present his proposal.[8]

Johnson was not the only person wanting legislation that would expand use of electricity. Many others were pushing the same arguments—more extension of transmission lines into rural areas. Under such persuasions, FDR became convinced that private utility companies would not do the job at rates country people could afford. The federal government would have to lead the way. As a department, REA had been an executive decision, but it was time to turn it into law.

Accordingly, Senator George Norris of Nebraska and Representative Sam Rayburn of Texas offered a bill directing the existing REA Department that when making loans it was to give preference to nonprofit agencies such as farmers' cooperatives. The funds could then be used to build transmission lines. Congress passed the bill, and it became law on May 20, 1936.

REA moved forward rapidly and eventually brought electricity to millions of homes. By 1937, despite the Depression, 1.25 million farms had electric power— 500,000 more than in 1934. In the dismal year of 1934, only one out of every ten farms had electricity; by 1950, nine out ten enjoyed it.

Farm life, hitherto dark, drab, and backbreaking, was in a miraculous new decade, and REA had helped usher it in.

BOOK II: STORMS APPROACHING
CHAPTER 17: WARNING CLOUDS

World War I had awakened a crusading spirit across America. The country had gone to war under the slogan of making "the world safe for democracy," and by 1920 President Woodrow Wilson, although still in the White House, was ill and with diminished executive powers.

Following the slaughter of the war, isolationist sentiment had swept over America, shaping strategies and policies of both national parties. A dozen years after World War I ended, many Americans remained convinced that arms and munitions makers were responsible for a foreign war which we had no business getting into in the first place.

Disillusioned with European politics, Americans had rejected both the peace treaty and the League of Nations and in 1928 had given overwhelming support to the Kellogg-Briand Pact, which supposedly outlawed aggressive war. The cult of neutrality continued to swell to unrealistic proportions; Wilson's dreams evaporated and were replaced with hope to trade with all nations but to avoid alliances with any of them. Individual citizens and organized groups warned government officials to be on guard against slick Europeans who had misled the country once before and would try to do so again.

Isolationism was fueled further by uncritical acceptance of reports from Senate investigators spurred by Gerald P. Nye of North Dakota. Senator Nye and fellow committeemen disclosed that, throughout World War I, dealers in arms and munitions had amassed exorbitant profits and by seamy tactics had avoided paying taxes. Moreover, isolationist temperaments during the 1930s permitted the depredations of Adolph Hitler and Benito Mussolini to go unchecked. The two dictators swallowed independent governments in Europe and Africa. Americans, British, and French expressed shock and outrage but chose not to get involved.

As the Great Depression worsened in the United States and poverty gripped the nation, citizens again searched for causes and scapegoats. Some attributed the disaster to the fact that all over the world economies were in shambles; others castigated the avarice of millionaires and Wall Street brokers, and many blamed minority groups—Jews, Asiatics, blacks, or international conspiracies—led by

Bolshevists and other "hyphenated Americans."

The roaring twenties spawned lawlessness, and larger cities had boasted of speakeasies and gangsters. There were countless constitutional violations, usually followed by irrational defenses. In Central Washington, radicals shot down Armistice Day paraders and patriotic citizens in revenge took a white citizen—admittedly a member of Industrial Workers of the World, the IWW (derisively called "I Won't Work" by many Americans)—out of jail and hanged him before throwing his body off a bridge.

In cities, jobless, dispirited men and women gathered in tight knots around speakers who stood on park benches or soapboxes and harangued about failures in the capitalist system, the greed of employers and bosses with their big homes uptown, the need for working men and women to unite, and to claim their rights. "There's no unemployment in the Soviet Union, comrades," declared speakers. "And there wouldn't be any here either if we workers owned the means of production."

In the aftermath of the First World War, America had survived the alleged Red Menace and the attacks upon it led by U.S. Attorney General A. Mitchell Palmer. Under provisions of the drastic war-time Sedition Act, Palmer as chief legal officer of the Administration cooperated with the Secretary of Labor in rounding up communists or suspected ones, bundling them off to jail, and later deporting many to Russia.

The U.S. had been in a diplomatic stand-off with Russia since 1917, when relations with the Kerensky regime, successor to the Czar's control, were rejected. Sixteen years afterwards, in November 1933, President Franklin Roosevelt renewed official relations with the Soviet Union, receiving a disavowal from Soviet Premier Josef Stalin that the Communist Party in America was supported by the governing group in Russia. This action by the new president had not been implemented without protests, including disapprovals from the President's mother and her friends as well as some of his own.

Father Edmund Walsh, rector of Georgetown University and an occasional advisor to FDR at the time, revealed that before taking the step Roosevelt had invited him to the White House where the President disclosed his intention to recognize the Soviet Government.

"Don't do it, Mr. President. Don't do it," the Catholic father remonstrated. "It will be the biggest mistake you could make."

"Don't worry, Father," Roosevelt smiled his reply. "I'm a good horse trader."[1]

Less dangerous but equally bitter as the Communists in launching criticisms was the Socialist Party in America during the Great Depression. In contrast with Communists and Fascists, however, Socialists did not urge quick overthrow of governing forces but preached instead that evolutionary socialism would eventually come about.

In New York, members of the State Assembly expelled fellow members because they had been voted in as representatives from the dreaded Socialist Party, thereby disenfranchising all their constituents. The Vice President of the United State rebuked women debaters from venerable Radcliffe College because they upheld the affirmative side of the proposition: *Resolved, that recognition of labor unions by employers is essential to successful collective bargaining.*[2]

Norman Mattoon Thomas had inherited the Socialist leadership mantle after the death of Eugene V. Debs in 1924. Thomas, a Princeton graduate, served as a Presbyterian pastor, and was a pacifist during WWI. He joined the Socialist Party during that conflict, and after it ended became editor first of the *World Tomorrow* and then the *Nation*.

As a student at Princeton University, Thomas was especially active in competitive debate, and he recalled a formal contest there over which President Woodrow Wilson had presided. All participants wore academic gowns, and Thomas remembered: "As we were about to go in, Mr. Wilson looked at my legs, and where the gown stopped, observed my gray trousers—they were pressed—and he said, 'Mr. Thomas, it is proper to wear dark trousers.' In spite of that I won the debate."[3]

A prolific writer and brilliant platform orator, Thomas would become a perennial presidential candidate, first running for that office in 1928 and again in 1932. In the last-named year he polled 190,000 votes and was on the ballot for the presidency four more times afterwards before his death in 1968.

One of the founders of what became the American Civil Liberties Union, Thomas opposed America's entry into the second World War while denouncing fascism and dictatorship of the proletariat. In his advanced years, he was almost sightless, hard of hearing, and crippled by arthritis, but retained his keen interest in people and public affairs.

Thomas criticized U.S. actions in the Vietnam War but didn't like the sight of young people burning the American flag. Some loyalties were necessary in life he said, adding, "If they want an appropriate symbol, they ought to be *washing* it, not *burning* it."

Not long after his eighty-fourth birthday, Thomas died in his sleep at home in Marion, Ohio.

Small wonder that Americans were fidgety on October 30, 1938, when Orson Welles broadcast his radio drama entitled "Invasion from Mars." The show, originally intended as a Halloween event, was an episode in an anthology series presented by the Mercury Theatre of the Air. Adapted from British novelist H. G. Wells' (no relation to Orson) novel *War of the Worlds*, the first two-thirds of the radio drama used a technique of news bulletins which suggested to many listeners that an actual Martian invasion was taking place. The resulting panic was reported around the world and even disparagingly mentioned by Hitler in a public speech.[4]

Despite the outcry against using the fake news bulletins, the broadcast launched Orson Welles to further radio and film fame.

Dominated by international economic troubles in the years following 1930, several European nations were teetering on the brink of bankruptcy. Such stresses led to dictators, and two of those—Adolph Hitler and Benito Mussolini—were bent on territorial expansion.

Chancellor Hitler, in the spring of 1934, formally denounced all disarmament clauses of the Treaty of Versailles. Alongside this public announcement came disclosure that Germany had reintroduced conscription and was increasing its army to thirty-six divisions. Later in that year, Mussolini, hoping to rekindle glories of ancient Rome, sent mechanized warriors into Africa and hapless Ethiopia. Citizens in the western world deplored that Italy "had resorted to war in disregard of obligations under former treaty agreements" but imposed no sanctions of any sort.

Hitler, in March 1937, violated the Treaty of Versailles and moved *Wehrmacht* troops into the Rhineland. At about the same time, civil war broke out in Spain, and in that fall a German-Italian Pact established the Berlin-Rome Axis. At the opening of the next year, Hitler, through Nazi manipulations, annexed all of Austria; France was docile, Italy was occupied with Mediterranean affairs, and the British reconciled themselves to the move. Emboldened and unchallenged by the Munich agreement, in September 1938, der Fuhrer did almost the same in dismembering Czechoslovakia. With that country entirely under German control as was true of Hungary and other Danubian countries, Germany now stood as the strongest power on the European continent.

When the *Wehrmacht* invaded Poland, a new European war was begun, which would last five and three-quarter years, demand nearly three hundred thousand lives of American men and women in uniform as well as an untold number of civilians. On Sept 5, 1939, four days after the Nazis invaded, President Roosevelt announced that U.S. would be neutral in European War.

As Germany undertook its purge of Jews, many of them emigrated to safer countries. Among those who came to America in the early years of the nineteen-thirties was the German physicist Albert Einstein. Born in Ulm, Germany, in 1879, Einstein had grown up in Munich. In schools he consistently had earned high marks, particularly in mathematics and Latin. He completed his Ph.D. at the University of Zurich and by 1907 the twenty-eight-year-old had published his first paper suggesting the theory of relativity. He was an associate professor at the University of Zurich before becoming a researcher in Berlin under the aegis of the Prussian Academy of Sciences. Einstein, in Berlin, began working with Max Planck, and he also met Leo Szilard, a theoretical physicist from Hungary. Einstein and Szilard became partners in practical inventions, and in the years between 1924 and 1934 the two of them had been awarded twenty-nine different patents, mostly dealing with refrigeration.

In 1921, Einstein was invited to come to the U.S., where he lectured at Columbia University, the City College of New York, and Princeton University. By this time he was wearing a mantle as one of the world's leading scientists. It would be twelve years (1933) before Einstein would emigrate to the U.S. and establish his residency as a professor at the Institute for Advanced Study in Princeton, N.J.

During his years in Berlin, Einstein had begun raising funds for the Zionist cause of a Hebrew university in Palestine, and along with his scientific accomplishments came recognition as a spokesman for Jewish causes. Returning to Europe in 1923, he found anti-Semitism rampant, particularly in Berlin and Munich; he considered both cities his home base.

Adolph Hitler, imprisoned at Landsberg after the Beer Hall Putsch of 1923, was writing *Mein Kampf* (My Struggle), and after his release from prison he continued his long-winded orations, giving vent to malevolence against Jews wherever he could capture listeners. Hitler's rantings were too much for Einstein and physicists in his coterie—Max Planck, Edward Teller, Eugene Wigner, Leo Szilard, Hans Geiger, and Niels Bohr.

Leo Szilard was a survivor of devastated Hungary after WWI, and alongside his record in physics he had developed a passion for human lives. Szilard had come to America where he met Enrico Fermi, an Italian physicist who had emigrated to the U.S. at about the same time. Both attended a conference in Washington, D.C., in April 1939, where Dr. Niels Bohr read a paper declaring that a small amount of pure Isotrope U235 of uranium with slow neutron particles of atoms would start a "chain reaction" sufficiently great to blow up a laboratory and many miles of countryside surrounding it.

The threat of nuclear bombs already had been planted in the minds of Szilard and Fermi, and Bohr's declaration confirmed the imminence. Together Szilard and Fermi drafted a petition advocating a demonstration of the power of nuclear bombs and shared it with their mentor Albert Einstein. The petition went through several drafts with minor alterations suggested by Edward Teller and Eugene Wigner, but the main idea remained.[5]

The scientists agreed that the proposal could best be presented to President Franklin Roosevelt if it came from someone outside their group. The man selected was Dr. Alexander Sachs, an economist who had contributed his knowledge to FDR on several occasions.

It was not until October 1939 that Sachs could get a private audience with FDR, and in that atmosphere he orally explained the idea of nuclear bombs, stressing that the concept was endorsed by Albert Einstein, the world's leading physicist.

After listening to Sach's oral explanation, FDR remarked, "Alex, what you are up to is to see that the Nazis don't blow us up."

"Precisely," Sachs replied.[6]

Within weeks the Manhattan Project was launched. Teams of physicists and chemists were chosen and contributing experiments undertaken at several prestigious universities. There was no public disclosure, and the work with its vast problems of coordination was known only to a few scattered scientists. Individual workers on the project had no knowledge of what it was about, and the Manhattan Project with its resultant atomic bomb became the most successful secret of World War II.

CHAPTER 18: AID TO BRITAIN

The First World War gave great impetus to use of motors and engines. Early tanks, considered behemoths at the time, were introduced and had clanked across the battlefields of Western Europe. Although field artillery was still drawn by horses, mules, and men, mounted horsemen were no longer of use and were replaced by trench warfare. From front lines, motorized ambulances marked with huge Red Crosses and carrying wounded, maimed men bounced their way backwards toward hospitals.

Air power, despite stirring accounts of deeds by aces like Eddie Rickenbacker and Manfred Richthofen, was not a pivotal factor in the war to save democracy. WWI had hardly ended, however, before militarists in former belligerent nations turned attention to air power. In America, pioneers like William "Billy" Mitchell, Henry "Hap" Arnold, and Curtis LeMay gave demonstrations to officials and politicians of what bombs dropped from airplanes could do—that is, destroy stationary targets or even ships on the sea. Even more spectacular, in 1927 one American pilot became hero to the civilized world.

On May 21, 1927, Charles A. Lindbergh took off in a small monoplane named *The Spirit of St. Louis*, piloting the craft from New York to Paris in a solo, nonstop, transatlantic passage. The feat captivated the world, and upon his return to tumultuous crowds in America, Lindbergh was promoted to colonel. Then he embarked on a nation-wide tour meant to spark more interest in aviation. Everywhere he went he was met by cheering crowds; there was no doubt, the epoch-making, solo flight across the Atlantic established Charles Lindbergh, *the Lone Eagle*, as the most idolized American of the 1920s.

Adolph Hitler boasted that he had been "elected" to leadership of Germany at about the same time Franklin Roosevelt had captured the presidency of the U.S. In truth, der Fuhrer never won a national election and only gathered his almost unanimous support from Germans and their minions after he was appointed Chancellor. Swastikas, banners, and Nazi slogans inexorably swarmed over European countries, and some Nazi adherents began combing America for recruits.

The German American Bund, (*Bund*—a German word for Federation) was a

Nazi organization in the U.S. during the 1930s. Its formation was an outgrowth of hostile competition between Jews and German businessmen in the neighborhood of Yorkville, Manhattan. The neighborhood there was heavily populated with German descendants who decided first to use propaganda in combating a Jewish-inspired boycott of their businesses. A U.S. Congressional inquiry looked into the dispute and announced that the American Germans were being supported by Nazi funds and, therefore, were a branch of Adolph Hitler's party.

After learning of this announcement, Hitler, hoping to gain some favor, asked all German nationals in the U.S. to withdraw from the tiny "Federation of Friends of New Germany" as the American group was called. In 1936, antipathies had worsened; the group's name was changed to German American Bund, and Hitler placed Fritz Julius Kuhn, American underling, at its head.

Taking cues from Propaganda Minister Josef Goebbels in the Third Reich, Kuhn used short films to promote the Bund's views. Near the close of 1936, he and fifty cohorts boarded a boat and sailed for Germany, hoping to gain attention and official recognition from Hitler himself during the Berlin Olympics. Kuhn did meet Hitler and later insisted that the Chancellor had designated him the "American Fuhrer." Actually, Herr Hitler had been less than enthusiastic. Perhaps he saw Kuhn as a rival or maybe he thought the time was not yet ripe. Regardless of his motivations, it was clear Hitler then wanted the American Bund to remain non-aggressive and relatively obscure.

After his return to America, Kuhn and his followers continued their siren songs, and the Bund swelled in numbers. Its highest point came on President's Day, February 19, 1939, when in New York City more than 20,000 people gathered in prestigious Madison Square Garden to hear Kuhn lambaste the American government. He repeatedly referred to President Franklin Roosevelt as "Frank D. Rosenfeld" and called his New Deal the "Jew Deal."

When Kuhn alleged that America's economic and political troubles stemmed from "Bolshevik-Jewish" leadership, a protester rushed the lectern. Police moved in to shield Kuhn and to lead him toward safety. The protester was hustled away, and violence erupted throughout the Garden. There were enough police to escort Kuhn and his supporters, together with their swastikas and banners, down the aisles and out of the building. Thus, the American Nazi was protected by the very forces he had been castigating.

Before the year 1939 ended, a New York tax investigation determined that Fritz Kuhn had embezzled monies from the Bund. Although that organization's charter had declared that its leader's powers were absolute, investigators chose to prosecute Kuhn nevertheless, knowing that regardless of the trial's outcome their efforts would cripple the Bund. It did that, and the effect, together with a "Christmas Declaration by men and women of German ancestry" signed by journalist Dorothy Thompson, Babe Ruth, and fifty other prominent citizens, spelled the doom of Fritz Kuhn and the German American Bund.

A nonaggression pact between the Nazis and the Soviets allowed Germany to attack neighboring Poland, and on the first day of September in 1939 Nazi troops crossed the Oder River to take over the Polish town of Gleiwitz. Britain and France had signed binding treaties with Poland guaranteeing that country's sovereignty, and in consequence both the western powers were forced to declare war on Germany.

Thus was begun a European war which would last five and three-quarter years, demand nearly three hundred thousand lives of American men and women in uniform, and an untold number of civilians. German bombs would kill 70,000 British citizens, and American and British bombers would destroy major targets throughout Germany and its satellites. The sneak attack on Pearl Harbor by Japanese later brought America into the war and spread the fighting into the Far East. By August, 1945 when all conflicts ended, lives of more than forty-five million persons would be sacrificed following that incursion by Germany in 1939.[1]

The Poles fought bravely, but their small army was hopelessly outdated. Cavalry and horse-drawn artillery was no match for German tanks and the *Luftwaffe*. Der Fuhrer sent five of his armies into Poland, and defenders there tried to protect far too much territory. Nazi pincer troops closed around seven different border areas before *Panzers* broke through to the rear, preventing the Poles from establishing defense lines along the Vistula River. Then, less than three weeks after Germans invaded Gleiwitz, Soviet troops from the east poured into the hapless country. Caught between the two aggressors, Poland's fate was sealed. Three days before the month of September ended, Poland capitulated, and German occupation began

Not long after Russia had seized eastern Poland, Soviet troops attacked Finland and captured the Baltic states. Hitler put out peace feelers to Britain and France but was rebuffed. The Western Front settled down into a stalemate that became known as the "phony war" or "*sitzkrieg*" as both sides awaited the coming of spring.

In the spring, German forces staged blitzkrieg assaults on Denmark, Norway, and the Low Countries. Throughout America there was an air of complacence; conventional wisdom held that Germans would be unable to pierce the Maginot Line extending along the French border from Switzerland to Belgium. Fast-moving German mobile units, however, easily went around the touted Maginot Line, entered France, and captured its capital city in June 1940.

In May of 1940, Prime Minister Neville Chamberlain of England had been replaced by Winston Churchill, who promised his countrymen nothing but "blood, toil, sweat, and tears." Across the Atlantic, President Franklin Roosevelt believed that, despite the Luftwaffe's bombings and onslaughts by Nazi U-boats, Britain would be able to maintain control of the seas. Germany would be strangled, and the U.S. need not get actively involved.

Five days after he became prime minister, Winston Churchill sent FDR a desperate request for fifty or sixty destroyers. Private correspondence between the two continued until September 5, 1940, when the agreement to transfer fifty "overaged" destroyers was completed. Churchill would tell the House of Commons that "by the long arm of coincidence" the destroyers already were in ports where they could be turned over immediately to British crews.

As Adolph Hitler moved toward further expansion of the Third Reich in the spring and summer of 1939, President Roosevelt stepped up his arguments that the arms embargo actually encouraged Germany and that it was in America's best interests to send arms to Britain and France. Governments of the two latter countries had signed pacts with Poland and Romania guaranteeing them against aggression. Poland, on Germany's eastern border, was especially vulnerable, and Romania had been included because its refineries produced one-third of Hitler's high-octane aviation gasoline, panzer fuel, benzene, and lubricants. From there would come more than half the oil that later kept Rommel's armor running on the sand plains of Mediterranean Africa. Hitler, his appetite whetted by ingestion of Austria and Czechoslovakia, turned hungry eyes toward neighboring Poland.

In Washington, President Roosevelt, in a private meeting with key legislators during the summer of 1939, tried to drum up support for Britain and France. A majority of those present were not convinced by his arguments, however. Senator Borah of Idaho insisted he had private information assuring him there would be no European war. Vice President Garner ended the discussion by saying, "Well, Captain, we may as well face the facts. You haven't got the votes, and that's all there is to it."[2] Meanwhile, France equivocated, Neville Chamberlain's government in Britain fiddled, and Poland quibbled.

Then on August 24, 1939, the standoff in Europe took a sudden turn for the worse when Soviet Premier Josef Stalin did an about-face and signed a peace treaty with Hitler. Western diplomats were stunned, for the two dictators had been abusing each other for the past five years. Now this new pact promised each of them non-aggression and included secret clauses for the partition of Poland. The way was clear for further German conquests.

At dawn on September 1, 1939, Nazi armed forces crossed the Oder River to take over the Polish town of Gleiwitz, and soon after midnight on that day, American ambassadors in Warsaw and Paris were able to relay news of the invasion to President Roosevelt. At a hastily called press conference the next day, the inevitable question arose, "Can we stay out?" FDR kept repeating, "I believe so . . . every effort will be made by this Administration to do so."[3]

Two days later, FDR gave a fireside chat to the American people. His message was carefully crafted in order to win public support and at the same time not unduly rile isolationist factions.

This nation will remain a neutral nation, but I cannot ask that every American remain neutral in thought as well. Even a neutral has a right to take account of facts. Even a neutral cannot be asked to close his mind or his conscience. . .

I hope the United States will keep out of this war. I believe it will. And I give you assurance and reassurance that every effort of your Government will be directed toward that end.[4]

Roosevelt must have felt compelled to make such dissembling, if not actually misleading, statements in order to bolster support for repeal of the arms embargo. Two weeks later he called Congress into a special session, and a month-long fight ensued. Congressmen were flooded with letters and telegrams urging repeal or warning against it. Isolationists insisted that FDR was planning "to send the boys of American mothers to fight on the battlefields of Europe," but the president countered by meeting daily with individual senators and by using all his personal persuasions to bring them around to his side.

After a month of behind-the-scenes meetings in the White House, the Senate went along and repealed the arms embargo by a vote of sixty-three to thirty. The House followed suit a few days later. President Roosevelt had won another tremendous debate.

By the opening of 1940, Roosevelt and Churchill were not yet personal friends; the two had met only casually in 1918. However, two weeks after Germany invaded Poland, President Roosevelt had written the Britisher a warm note of congratulation upon his being returned to the Admiralty and inviting further confidential correspondence.

With the arms embargo repealed and relations with Britain growing ever closer, FDR, in January 1941, told aide Harry Hopkins that many of the problems in supplying the Western Allies could be settled if only he and Churchill could meet privately. Hopkins set about arranging details for such a confab in the coming August at Placentia Bay, lying at the tip of land, about 800 miles northeast of Boston. It was the first face-to-face meeting between the President and the Prime Minister, establishing a pattern of wartime get-togethers of Allied leaders.

Churchill came to Placentia Bay as a suitor, using all his powers of persuasion to get a reluctant American bride to the altar. His aim was to draw the American navy across the Atlantic so that a clash with Germany was bound to come. Hitler either would have to hold back U-boat attacks in the Atlantic for fear of sinking American ships or he would risk bringing America into the war.

Meeting aboard ships in Placentia Bay had given the two leaders an opportunity to measure one another. Judged from that perspective, the meeting was successful, for their conference began a friendship which would direct the war and shape subsequent peace structures. Privately, Churchill described FDR as a "charming country gentleman," which might be translated as a bit of lightweight. Sir Alexander Cadogan, one of Churchill's advisors, reported that at a dinner on August 9, the American President had entertained all with descriptions of his Hyde Park estate, where he hoped to grow Christmas trees for the market. And Roosevelt came back to Washington impressed by Churchill's qualities of mind, his easy banter, and his command of language.

Later, during a cabinet meeting in Washington, Roosevelt was advised to beware of Churchill's skills as a persuader, and FDR replied with smugness similar to what he had given when warned about Soviet Russia—"But of course, you know, Grandpa's pretty good at trading, too."[5]

Out of this conference between Roosevelt and Churchill off the coast of Newfoundland came the Atlantic Charter, one of the most compelling statements of the war. The wording of the broad postwar principles of the U.S. and Britain laid down at the historic meeting was idealistic and sententious, but such were inspiring and gave guidance for future collaborations. At conclusion of the meeting, a document was released which included these premises: 1) renunciation of territorial or other aggrandizement, 2) opposition to territorial changes contrary to the wishes of the people immediately concerned, 3) support of the right of peoples to choose their own form of government, 4) support, with due respect for existing obligations, of the easing of restrictions on trade and access to raw materials on equal terms, 5) support of cooperative efforts to improve the economic position and social security of the peoples of the world, 6) freedom from want and fear, 7) freedom of the seas, and 8) disarmament of aggressor nations pending the establishment of a permanent peace structure.[6]

In addition to broad goals agreed upon during the conference were significant strategic decisions and military commitments. The British were bent on bombing, blockading, and wearing down Germany; American military leaders, particularly George Marshall, contended it would be necessary for Allied ground forces to invade the Continent and close with the enemy before Germany could be defeated.

Churchill pressed for stepped-up American action in the Atlantic, and FDR agreed to provide American escorts for all fast convoys between Newfoundland and Iceland. Churchill disclosed that Britain planned to seize and occupy the Canary Islands lying off the coast of northwestern Africa—a move that no doubt would lead to Spain's counterattack with aid from the Nazis. Later, the British scrapped plans for seizure of the Islands, but Roosevelt's willingness to support the Azores shows how far even then he was ready to stretch neutrality interpretations.

Upon his return to Washington, FDR found a sobering piece of news awaiting him. The House had passed a bill previously approved by the Senate to extend Selective Service for six months. Passage of the act had been exceedingly close—203 votes to 202. One leading opponent, Senator Wheeler, had mailed a million postcards advising recipients: "*Write to President Roosevelt today that you are against our entry into the European war.*" Resistance to the bill was one of the isolationists' last large-scale and organized efforts.

As more Allied ships sailed the Atlantic and more Nazi U-boats patrolled those waters, there were bound to be incidents. One occurred on September 4, 1941, when a U-boat fired two torpedoes at the *U.S.S. Greer*, a destroyer on duty in waters off the coast of Iceland. There had been considerable provocation, for the *Greer* had trailed the sub for three hours, acting as a spotter for a British patrol plane. The two torpedoes missed their target, but President Roosevelt prepared to make the most of the incident. He was working on a speech to report it but was interrupted by news that his mother, Sara Roosevelt, had died.

After Sara's funeral, FDR, on September 11, 1941, wearing a black mourning band on his light seersucker suit, gave his "shoot on sight" fireside chat. In it he compared Adolph Hitler to a uniquely American creature:

When you see a rattlesnake poised to strike, you do not wait until he has struck you before you crush him. . . From now on if German or Italian war vessels enter the waters, the protection of which is necessary for American defenses, they do so at their own peril.[7]

Other attacks followed the Greer incident. In the second week of October, a forty-ship convoy 400 miles south of Iceland ran into a wolf pack. Three ships were torpedoed, and more were being picked off, when a rescue force of five American destroyers out of Reykjavik arrived. By then it was dark. The *U.S.S. Kearney* was hit by a torpedo but made it back to Iceland. Eleven crewmen had been killed, and the first American blood had been spilled.

News of that attack arrived in Washington while the Senate was debating FDR's proposed amendments to the Neutrality Act—amendments already passed by the House. The President wanted to arm American merchantmen and send them all the way into British ports. Isolationists clamored against the move. Senator Robert A. Taft of Ohio declared the Neutrality Act was the sole safeguard keeping America out of the war. Arguments were frequent and emotional; nevertheless, the amendments passed the Senate in the last of October, and American vessels were permitted to carry arms into British ports.

CHAPTER 19: CAMPAIGN OF 1940

The executive power shall be vested in a President of the United States of America. He shall hold his office during the term of four years, and, together with the Vice President, chosen for the same term, be elected as follows . . . Thus reads the beginning of Article II, Section 1 of the Constitution.

Nothing in that Article or thereafter in the Constitution set a limit on how many terms a President might serve. George Washington, the first person to win the office and the patriot who more than any other held the infant nation together, established a precedent not ignored for nearly a 150 years.

After seven years of leading a struggling infant government, Washington announced his irrevocable decision to return to Mt. Vernon at the end of his second term. He was followed by twenty-eight different men, none of whom, until the advent of Franklin Roosevelt in 1933, aspired for more than eight years as the nation's Chief Executive. Events on the world stage during the last half of the 1930s may have helped Roosevelt make his precedent-shattering decision.

The court-packing controversy soured relations between FDR and many of his key supporters in Congress, and as a result legislative matters during the early months of 1937 were brought to a virtual standstill. The only accomplishment of note was enactment of two revised neutrality laws: 1) emergency legislation to embargo shipment of arms to both sides in Spain's civil war, and 2) the Neutrality Act of 1937.

In 1935, as FDR prepared for another four-year-term, the Spanish civil war—a squall line forerunning the storm of World War II—was in its second year. In America, there was an outgrowth of widespread isolationist sentiment. In 1935 and 1936, Congress had passed a scissors-and-paste combination of resolutions mandating an arms embargo if the President found a state of war existing anywhere. The resolutions also prohibited the sale of arms and munitions to either side in such conflict.

At the beginning of FDR's second administration, isolationists had momentum. Congress passed a revised Neutrality Act May 1, 1937, although the revised act retained many provisions of the earlier law—mandatory arms embargo, a ban on loans and credits to belligerents, a ban on travel by Americans on belligerent ships, and prohibition from arming American ships trading with belligerents. The biggest change in the new law was giving the President authority to put the sale of non-embargoed goods to belligerents on a cash-and-carry basis—that is, the goods had to be transferred to American hands and be carried to belligerents in non-American ships.

Meanwhile, Adolph Hitler had rebuilt his armies and air forces so rapidly that he was ready to embark upon a course of conquest. In February he forced the collapse of the Austrian government, and a month later German troops made their triumphant entry into Vienna. Control of Austria placed neighboring Czechoslovakia in the jaws of a Nazi vise. Czechs were ready to resist, but Western nations demurred and pushed for peace at almost any price.

In September, British Prime Minister Neville Chamberlain and French Premier Edouard Daladier met with Hitler and Mussolini in Munich. Agreements the four made permitted Germany to set new frontiers for Czechoslovakia and to conduct a plebiscite for a new government. No Czechs were permitted to attend the conference, and essentially the "agreement" was nothing more than acceptance of an ultimatum der Fuhrer had laid down earlier.

"This is the last territorial claim I have to make in Europe," Hitler declared. Prime Minister Chamberlain returned to cheering crowds in London and announced, "This is the second time there has come back from Germany peace with honour. I believe it is peace in our time."

In April 1939, FDR sent Hitler and Mussolini an extraordinary public letter which was broadcast to all parts of the world. "Are you willing," asked the American President, "to give assurance that your armed forces will not attack or invade the territory or possessions of thirty-one specific nations?"

Reacting to Roosevelt's ploy, Mussolini sneered that the request was "the result of infantile paralysis!"[1]

Hitler's response was even more insulting. Convening the Reichstag, he shouted, "If all problems could be solved around a conference table, why had the United States rejected the League of Nations? If Germans had asked about American intentions in Latin America they most certainly would have been told to mind their own business." Furthermore, der Fuhrer maintained that each of the thirty-one states mentioned in FDR's message had been asked if it felt threatened by Germany; all replies had been negative. He ranted further, with each sarcastic thrust drawing roars of malicious laughter.

Isolationists in America noted Hitler's and Mussolini's responses to Roosevelt's naiveté, and Senator Hiram Johnson of California wrote to his son, "Hitler had all the better of the argument.... Roosevelt put his chin out and got a resounding whack. I have reached the conclusion that there will be no war."[2]

In that summer and fall, while Roosevelt was doing all he could to help the British, he also had to campaign for reelection. In deciding to run for a third term, FDR had broken tradition, and he faced a formidable opponent in Wendell Wilkie.

Wilkie's candidacy raised Republican hopes everywhere, and indeed in the November election he garnered more popular votes than any Republican in history, but in Franklin Roosevelt he was up against the most masterful politician the country had ever known. Moreover, with the black horse of hunger, despair, and poverty being chased into the past either through war scares or New Deal measures, FDR was at the height of his power and prestige. The popular vote was relatively close, but the electoral vote was more decisive: 449 to 82.

By mid-December the British had nearly exhausted their financial resources. Relations between Churchill and Roosevelt had become more intimate as increasingly more letters and telegrams were exchanged. An outgrowth was a "brain wave" credited to FDR by Lord Maynard Keynes. The idea was that war materials would be more useful to the defense of the *United States* (emphasis supplied by author) than if they were kept in storage in the U.S. President Roosevelt used a homely metaphor when he announced the plan to the public:

What I am trying to do is to eliminate the dollar sign. Suppose my neighbor's home catches fire, and I have a length of garden hose four or five hundred feet away. If he can take my garden hose and connect it up with his hydrant, I may help him put out the fire. Now what do I do? I don't say to him before that operation, "Neighbor, my garden hose cost me $15; you have to pay me $15 for it." What is the transaction that goes on? I don't want $15—I want my garden hose back after the fire is over.[3]

On the night FDR gave this talk, Nazi Luftwaffe subjected London to one of its heaviest bombings. FDR's talk that night, however, captured headlines and was pivotal, including a phrase long remembered. "Arsenal of democracy" had been coined by Jean Monnet, a French representative then in Washington, and Supreme Court Justice Felix Frankfurter passed the term on to the President Roosevelt, who to Americans urged: "We must become the great arsenal of democracy. . . No dictator, no combination of dictators, will weaken that determination by threats of how they will construe that determination."[4]

The Democratic Party had healed most of the wounds over fights with the Supreme Court about Social Security and the NRA and organized a united front. The bill growing from FDR's "brain wave" and pushed by avid supporters was one of his irrevocable acts to which he committed himself and the nation prior to the bombing of Pearl Harbor.

The Lend-Lease Act (patriotically numbered H.R. 1776) was passed by Congress in March 1941 and in effect set up a de facto alliance between the U.S. and Hitler's foes.

When campaigning in the U. S. for the 1940 campaign got underway, the nation, and especially the Republican Party, was deeply divided. On one side were isolationists, or those who felt the nation should avoid helping any of the warring powers and avoid legislation that could bring America into the war. Opposing them were interventionists, who felt America's survival depended upon helping the British and other allied powers defeat Nazi Germany.

Republicans held their nominating convention in Philadelphia, and three stalwarts were leading the pack seeking top place on the ticket. Senator Taft of Ohio, Senator Arthur Vandenburg of Michigan, and Thomas E. Dewey, the vigorous, gang-busting Attorney General from Manhattan. One thousand delegates came to the Republican Convention, but only three hundred had pledged to a candidate; the road was clear for a challenger.

By the time the Republican Convention opened, across America sympathy for embattled Britain was mounting, but so was the opposition. Conservative Taft argued that America needed to stop the New Deal from capitalizing on the international crisis to extend socialism at home, and in New York, Republican Congressman Hamilton Fish III warned citizens that President Roosevelt had become Winston Churchill's accomplice; Roosevelt was making the country vulnerable to communism by enacting measures certain to bring the U.S. into war against Germany. As convention delegates began arriving in Philadelphia, Gallup Poll reported that support for Thomas Dewey had slipped to 47 percent, and support for Taft, Vandenberg, and Former President Hoover had fallen to 8 percent, 8 percent, and 6 percent respectively. The declines were due to the rise of the newcomer.

Wendell L. Wilkie had been born and raised in Indiana, earned his law degree from Indiana University, and, after serving as an officer in WWI, began his career as a corporate lawyer. In 1929—the year of the crash—he was named legal counsel for the New York-based Commonwealth & Southern Corporation, the nation's largest electric utility holding company. The Tennessee Valley Authority (TVA), the agency created by New Dealers in 1933, brought the government into direct competition with existing private power companies, including Commonwealth & Southern. The confrontation forced Wilkie to become an active critic of TVA as well as other New Deal agencies competing with private corporations. His main argument was that agencies such as TVA could charge cheaper rates than private businesses because they did not have to make a profit. Also, the government could borrow unlimited funds at low interest rates—rates far below those on which private corporations had to draw. Wilkie's Commonwealth & Southern could not compete and in 1939 was forced to sell its properties in the TVA regions for $78.6 million. Wilkie continued to make speeches, write editorials, and engage in debates attacking government intrusions into private businesses, and thus by 1940 was prominent in Republican circles.

Never before 1940 had Wendell Wilkie run for public office, but very quickly telegrams urging him to seek the presidency began to pour in. Petitions supporting him appeared everywhere, and among his backers were such powerful media magnates as Ogden Reid of the *New York Herald Tribune*, Roy Howard of the Scripps-Howard newspaper chain, and John and Gardner Cowles, publishers of the *Minneapolis Star* and the *Minneapolis Tribune*, as well as the *Des Moines Register* and *Look* magazine. At the very opening of the convention in Philadelphia, Governor Harold Stassen of Minnesota, the keynote speaker, announced for Wilkie, and the galleries went wild. Throughout the hall came gusty shouts of "We Want Wilkie! We Want Wilkie!" Nevertheless, six ballots had to be taken before the nomination for Indiana's favorite son was secured. Contrary to custom, the rookie candidate did not opt to select his own running mate but left that choice to the delegates, who picked Senate Minority Leader Charles L. McNary of Oregon for the second place.

An articulate debater, Wilkie's campaign in that fall of 1940 centered on three major themes: 1) the alleged inefficiency and corruption of New Deal programs, 2) FDR's attempt to win a third term was unprecedented and against established policy, and 3) the administrations' lack of military preparedness. Wilkie said that as President he would retain some New Deal programs but would make them more efficient and merge them with private business leaders to end the Great Depression.

No issue, however, fired the public as much as the threat of being dragged into the European war. Wilkie hammered on FDR's lack of military preparedness, but the President blunted the blows by expanding military contracts and instituting the military draft. The Phony War had ended in April 1940, and a month later Nazi troops rumbled triumphantly through the Low Countries: Holland, Belgium, and Luxembourg. France was the next victim.

Italy's dictator, Benito Mussolini, watching the Nazi blitzkrieg, knew he could not delay much longer if he hoped to share in the spoils, so on June 10, he strutted onto his balcony in Rome's Piazza Venetia to announce that he, too, was sending troops into France.

Roosevelt received news of this announcement just an hour before he left Washington for a speech at the University of Virginia in Charlottesville. There, speaking in his habitual slow rate for emphasis and in a voice heavy with contempt, he declared, "On this tenth day of June 1940, the hand which held the dagger has struck it into the back of its neighbor."[5]

Wire photos four days later showed Germans entering Paris and victorious Nazi troops parading in the Place de la Concorde. Americans watched the momentous scenes with a growing sense of foreboding. Public opinion, strongly shaped by FDR's rhetoric and that of interventionist committees, began shifting away from the isolationists.

Wilkie was not an isolationist, and his candidacy buoyed Republican hopes, but he was facing an incumbent president at the height of his power and prestige and the most masterful politician the country had ever known.

FDR ran a campaign orchestrated by advisors, and he made relatively few speeches. However, he did tour New England states after which he declared, "I've had a glorious day in New England." He seldom attacked Wilkie directly, although on the evening of October 8, 1940, before a packed house in Madison Square Garden, he showed his mastery of political ridicule.

The campaign had intensified, and three of the leading Republican isolationists were Representatives Joseph Martin, the house majority leader and Wilkie's campaign manager, Bruce Barton, who was running for senator from New York, and Hamilton Fish, the archconservative congressman from the President's own Dutchess County district. "Martin, Barton, and Fish!" the names had a Wynken, Blynken, and Nod nursery rhyme cadence. When FDR recited them, his listeners howled with laughter. That night and in speeches thereafter, whenever FDR would intone, "I still remember that my opponent was once a member of that great triumvirate, Martin . . ." Even before he could follow with *Barton* and *Fish*, listeners would take up the chant and supply the name of Wilkie's former corporate partners. After the election had been decided, Wilkie said, "When I heard the President hang the isolationist votes of *Martin, Barton,* and *Fish* on me, I knew I was licked."[6]

Wilkie was an honorable opponent and excellent extempore speaker, but his campaign was plagued by small disasters. Not equipped nor trained for leather-lunged, continuous oratory, his voice gave out; nevertheless, he continued to croak his way across the country. Despite ointments, treatments, and gargling, his voice could not stand the strain, and in Illinois, he could manage only: *"The spirit is—* — (unintelligible sound), *but the voice has* –(similar unintelligible croak)."

As in most campaigns, there were dirty tricks. Republicans continued their calumnies against FDR: the smile on "That Man's" face had been grafted there by a plastic surgeon; he never earned a nickel in his life but lives off his mother's income; his family was essentially Jewish—the name originally was *van Rosenfeld*, and the oft-told story of a psychiatrist who died and arrived in heaven with delusions of grandeur—immediately sent to God, the newcomer treats Him haughtily because he regards himself as Franklin Roosevelt.

Wilkie, too, was subject to slander and ridicule. Some Republican stalwarts rejected him because he once had been a registered Democrat. Blue collar toughs booed him, and an egg hit his wife standing by his side. One distinguished historian of the Depression Era has written that nearly all of the Democratic abuse fired at Wilkie was unwarranted.[7] Supporters once tried to get a Wilkie endorsement from a Republican Senator who turned them down, snorting,

If a whore repented and wanted to join the church, I'd personally welcome her and I'd lead her up the aisle to a pew, but by the Eternal I'd not ask her to lead the choir the first night.[8]

Wilkie endorsed sending arms to Great Britain, refused to fault the destroyer deal, and believed the peacetime draft was necessary. Far from being a "Me-too" candidate, in truth he supported many FDR programs. He attacked New Deal measures because they intruded into private businesses. The Democratic candidate for the vice-presidency, Henry Wallace, fired some of the most vicious allegations, charging that Wilkie was the Nazis' first choice.

Late in the campaign Republicans discovered a series of letters Henry Wallace had written to a Russian mystic named Nicholas Foerich. In the letters Wallace addressed Foerich as "Dear Guru" and signed his own name as "G" for Galahad— the title Roerich had given him as a member of the faith. In the letters, Wallace assured his Russian correspondent that there would be "a breaking of the New Day," when the people of "Northern Shambella" (a Buddhist term roughly equivalent to the kingdom of heaven) would establish an era of peace and plenty. Upon learning the letters had been discovered, Democratic politicos were extremely fearful that if they became public and Wallace's eccentricities were exposed the ticket would be in jeopardy. Indeed, Republicans did threaten to reveal the letters, but put the idea aside when Democrats retaliated by insisting they would release information about Wilkie's rumored extramarital affair with writer Irita Van Doren.[9] The twin threats worked, and neither scandal surfaced until well after the election had been decided.

In the November election of 1940 Roosevelt received 449 electoral votes,

Wilkie 82. Apart from Maine and Vermont, Republicans carried only the isolationist heartland of the Midwest, but Wilkie did garner 45 percent of the popular vote. The two-term tradition established by the nation's first President and all followers had been shattered. Not until 1947 when Congress passed a bill, duly ratified three years later, limiting the President to two terms, were voters able to exact posthumous revenge upon FDR.

Wilkie did gain over six million more votes than the GOP's 1936 nominee, Al Landon, and he took 57 percent of the farm vote, but with the exception of Cincinnati FDR carried every city in the nation with a population of more than 400,000.

CHAPTER 20: EVE OF INFAMY

War in Europe had been going on for a year when in September 1940, Japanese representatives went to Berlin and signed a three-power pact. The treaty with Germany and Italy provided for a ten-year military and economic alliance. In the pact, which made Japan a member of the Axis, each signatory pledged mutual assistance in the event of war with a nation not then a belligerent. Subsequently, Nazi satellite governments, Bulgaria, Romania, Hungary, and Yugoslavia, endorsed the formal agreement.

In the last month of 1940, the Office of Production Management in the U. S., with William S. Knudsen as director, was set up by President Roosevelt. The purpose of the agency was to coordinate defense production and speed all material aid "short of war" to Great Britain and other anti-Axis nations. In the same month, talks in Washington by U. S. and British military staffs produced a secret strategic plan in case America was to be drawn into war with Germany and Japan. If that happened, it was agreed the concentration of force should first be on Germany.

Three months into the next year, one of the most momentous legislative acts of the crucial period, Lend Lease, was passed by Congress and approved by President Roosevelt. The Lend Lease Act was drawn up to offset the exhaustion of British credits for the purchase of war supplies. The Senate passed the measure, 60 to 31, and the House followed suit three days later with a vote of 317-71. The Lend Lease Act enabled any country whose defense the President deemed vital to that of the U. S. to receive arms, equipment, and other supplies by sale, transfer, exchange, or lease. An initial appropriation of $7 billion was authorized, and a total of $50,226,845,387 had been spent by the time Lend Lease was ended abruptly on May 8, 1945 by FDR's successor, President Harry S Truman.[1]

In the year of 1941, Europe was not the only continent darkened by war. The black horse of poverty and despair which had galloped across the land protected by two oceans no longer was the lead story in news reports. A red horse dominated reports from numerous places abroad and in the stretch was coming on strong toward America.

In the fall of 1938, only a scattered few had been concerned with the incursions of Japan, a predatory Empire whose army leaders in 1931 moved troops into the Chinese cities of Mukden, Ch'ang-ch'un, and Kirin. Nor were many Americans bothered the next year when Japan denounced all naval agreements made in 1921 and 1930. Government leaders in Washington, D.C. kept their eyes on Europe, where infections were bubbling into a genuine world boil.

In the Far East, Japanese onslaughts that had been marked with the rape of Nanking in 1937 continued almost unimpeded. With the forces of Britain and France desperately needed at home, the Empire of the Rising Sun saw a chance to achieve the goal of making all of Southeast Asia part of its autonomy.

Near the end of 1940, Joseph C. Grew, America's ambassador to Japan, returned to meet with President Roosevelt and to express concern over Japanese moves. FDR in response spoke confidently of intercepting the Japanese fleet if it moved southward, of reinforcing U.S. troops stationed in Manila and Pearl Harbor, and of impressive naval maneuvers soon to be displayed in the Pacific. He reiterated that it would continue to be U. S. policy to avoid confronting the Japanese while setting in place machinery to assist the British in Europe.

Ambassador Grew returned to Tokyo and there addressed a Japanese audience telling them that American public opinion resented Japanese aggression in China and that his government favored economic retaliation against further violations of American rights or international law. The ambassador's remarks received enthusiastic editorial endorsements in most of America, but there was no legislative or executive retaliation. Oil, gasoline, and finished steel continued to be sent to Japan. The Japanese, who depended on imports for 90 percent of their gasoline, were known to be stockpiling petroleum products, but throughout 1940 and the first half of 1941, when their intentions became more evident, American oil continued to be sold to them. The arsenal of democracy was the service station for fascism.

At the opening of 1941, Ambassador Grew sent Roosevelt an ominous report obtained from the Peruvian minister in Tokyo: "There is a lot of talk around town to the effect that the Japanese, in case of a break with the United States, are planning to go all out in a surprise mass attack on Pearl Harbor. I rather guess that the boys in Hawaii are not precisely asleep."[2] The State Department took no more notice of this message than it did to other similar warnings.

When American and British leaders met off the coast of Newfoundland in August 1941, Churchill wanted a hard line on Japan, too. He feared Japanese actions could leave Britain standing alone in Southeast Asia. Only the stiffest warning from America, he insisted, would have any deterrent effect on Japanese schemes.

Roosevelt demurred, however, saying he preferred to inform the Japanese that if they would pull out of Indochina, Washington would be able to settle remaining differences with them. Churchill had little alternative except to go along with the American president.

In May 1941, American intelligence agencies warned Washington that "Japan will strike soon," and experts decoded a message from Tokyo to Japan's foreign minister in Washington which read: "Should matters [American build-up vis 'a vis Japan] continue unchecked, Japan will be forced to live up to her obligations under the Japan-Germany-Italy Tripartite Pact."[3] Again, the administration in Washington took little heed of the warning.

When Japanese troops moved into southern Vietnam in July 1941, President Roosevelt acted by freezing Japanese funds in the United States and ordering an embargo of oil shipments to Japan. Great Britain and the Netherlands supported the U.S. action by cutting off Japan's source of credit in their respective nations and by forbidding any imports of rubber, scrap iron, and fuel oil. On the same day President Roosevelt had ordered the Japanese embargo, he accepted the armed forces of the Philippine Commonwealth into the United States Army and appointed General Douglas MacArthur to command all U.S. armed forces in the Far East.

Events were moving faster than American diplomats realized; war was all but inevitable. Americans thought they would have time to organize their army, strengthen the navy, and prepare for further defense of the Philippines, but unimpeded the Japanese were amassing their own land army and executing their naval push to the south.

The reigning government in Japan, headed by Fumimaro Konoye, fell in the second week of October 1941, and was replaced by an administration with General Hedeki Tojo, the fiercest hawk in the Orient, as prime minister. American Ambassador Joseph Grew wired from Tokyo that he felt FDR's hard line and refusal to negotiate had brought down the former regime and that its replacement was determined to go to war.

Within the month, General Tojo presented an ultimatum to the United States:

If the United States would stop reinforcing the Philippines, he would evacuate southern Indochina but would do so only if the U. S. would cut off aid to the Chinese forces led by Chiang Kai-shek and would "unfreeze" Japanese assets in the U. S.[4]

Such moves would leave the Japanese Empire free to complete its subjugation of China, so Tojo did not expect the U. S. to accept his terms—terms more appropriate for a defeated nation. His ultimatum was rejected, and Tojo along with other Japanese warlords ordered into action detailed plans laid earlier for aggression.

On November 17, 1941, the carrier fleet that would attack Hawaii left its bases for a secret rendezvous in the remote and sparsely inhabited Kurile Islands. In Washington, D.C. a special Japanese ambassador, Saburo Kurusu, arrived to reinforce the regular representative, Kichisaburo Nomura. The very next day, Kurusu and Nomura spent more than two hours with Secretary of State Cordell Hull, who knew from decoded Japanese messages that the Nipponese Empire was getting ready for war. The two Japanese envoys professed friendship for the United States but admitted relations were deteriorating. War would do neither nation any good, and both insisted they had come striving for peace.

On November 26, 1941, a Japanese striking force of six big aircraft carriers loaded with 423 planes, and escorted by two battleships, two heavy cruisers, and eleven destroyers, left from the rendezvous point in the Kurile Islands and headed for its fatal destination—Pearl Harbor.

The six carriers stopped 200 miles off Oahu, and pilots wearing white headbands lettered with *Hisso* (Certain Victory) climbed into cockpits of dive bombers, torpedo bombers, and pursuit planes before taking off to fly in formation east-ward—into the rising sun, the emblem of their nation. As the first plane roared down the deck of the flagship *Akagi*, sailors still aboard the vessel shouted three ceremonial *Banzais.*

FDR had attempted one last move to stem the inexorable drift toward war and had proposed an accommodation with the Japanese offering to return the situation in the Far East to the way it was in July 1941. The oil embargo imposed by the U.S. would be lifted, and talks between Japan and China initiated. In return, Japan would send no further troops to Indochina or along the Manchurian frontier with the Soviet Union. The American President wrote Churchill that he was not very "hopeful" that his offer would be accepted, and on the day after sending his British partner that message, FDR discussed with his War Council the possibility of a sur-prise Japanese attack. One of the attendees in the meeting that day, Secretary of War Henry Stimson, later wrote that in the discussion the President insisted that full support of the American people was absolutely necessary. Therefore, the U.S. would have to be blameless. Stimson observed, "The question was how we could maneuver *them* (the Japanese) into the position of firing the first shot without al-lowing too much danger to ourselves."[5]

FDR's try for a *modus vivendi* collapsed when the Chinese balked, fearing that any agreement with Japan would be at China's expense. War warnings accord-ingly were sent from Washington the next day to American commanders in the Pa-cific, including Admiral Husband E. Kimmel, commander of the Fleet at Pearl Harbor, and to General Walter Short, commander of the Hawaiian Department. Both were told that negotiations had broken down, and a Japanese attack could be expected on the Philippines, Thailand, or Borneo within the next few days.

On the evening of December 6, 1941, darkness had settled over Pearl Harbor. For men and women in uniform, Hawaii was the best assignment anyone could get. In barracks on land or in living quarters aboard ships, men had showered, shaved, shined shoes, and now were on shore leave bending elbows at bars or cud-dling girls on the dance floors of Honolulu. Mostly forgotten was the fact that Eu-rope had been at war for two years, and Japan was not thought of as a military threat.

In the space of less than twenty-four hours such idyllic scenes would be shat-tered. The history of the world would take a sudden change, and more than twenty-four hundred Americans would die.

For the past three years Japan had been seeking to control more oil and rubber from countries in Southeast Asia. After the mutual aid pact with Germany and Italy had been signed and concluded, planners in Tokyo were ready to add the military moves.

Leading the Tokyo administration were Admirals Yamamoto and Genda. In-telligence agents had told them and other Japanese militarists that almost the entire American Pacific Fleet was anchored in Pearl Harbor. Indeed, six battleships—pride of the U.S. Fleet: the *U. S. S. California, Maryland, Oklahoma, Tennessee, W. Virginia,* and *Nevada*—were in a row. The knowledge led Yamamoto to declare, "If we are to be successful we will have to destroy this fleet. It will then be at least six months before America can retaliate."

There were problems to overcome though; one was the depth of the channel. The channel leading into Pearl Harbor was too shallow for normal torpedoes. A combined attack—the brain child of Admiral Genda—had been devised. His plan called for an assault with bombs from the air at the same time Japanese midget submarines would launch newly-developed shallow-running torpedoes. The little submarines each carried only a two-man crew on what was certain to be a suicide mission. Each midget sub would sneak into the mouth of the harbor, and lurk on the bottom until planes began the actual attack; then the midgets could fire their torpedoes. Five of the little vessels approached the Island of Oahu.

Meanwhile, three hundred and fifty planes with big red suns emblazoned on fuselage and wings were launched from Japanese carriers. Aviators approaching Pearl Harbor could see sandy beaches, palm groves, lush vegetation, and rows of military barracks just as had been portrayed on maps and relief structures they had studied months beforehand.

A U. S. minesweeper, *The Condor*, spotted the periscope of one sub before the tiny ship submerged. Crew of the minesweeper wired the war office in Honolulu. Officers there received the message four hours before Japanese planes would arrive at Pearl Harbor but thought the minesweeper skipper had to be wrong, so nothing was done about it.

On Sunday morning in Hawaii at 6:30 A.M. there, officers aboard another American ship spied a second periscope. The U.S. vessel hurried toward it, but the periscope submerged before the American crew could get to the spot. Numerous depth charges from the guardian ship were hurled into the area where the sub was presumed to have been, and the American sailors were convinced they had sunk the unidentified sub. They wired accounts of the action to appropriate naval headquarters, but again no action was taken; the message slowly crept its way up the chain of command.

At 7:00 A.M. (Hawaiian time) planes flying at 5,000 feet approached Pearl Harbor from the north. Radar observers spotted them, but after calling in their report were told by a duty officer, "Don't worry about it." A third warning, but again nothing was done.

Yamamoto's plan called for two waves of airplane attacks. Each wave would take fifteen minutes to launch. The first wave would bomb Wheeler Air Field on Ford Island, and the second wave would hit battleships in Pearl Harbor itself.

At 7:53 A.M. in Hawaii (1:23 P.M. Washington time), the first Japanese torpedoes were launched, and the first bombs were released. Dive bombers attacked planes parked in rows wing tip to wing tip at the airfield, as well as buildings, gas tanks, and runways. At the same time, torpedo bombers went after battleship row in the nearby harbor. Bombs whistled and torpedoes exploded. One sailor at the naval base said later, "The damned Jap planes were so close you could throw rocks at 'em."

One battleship, the *U. S. S. Arizona,* tried to make it to the open sea, but armor-piercing Japanese bombs hit its major gun turrets. Almost instantly, 1,000 *Arizona* crewmen died, and oil from the ship began to flow and catch fire. Those still alive on the stricken vessel found themselves in an inferno. Thirty-five minutes after the air attack began, the planes flew away. In aftermath, 1,177 persons aboard the *Arizona* would die from the perfidious assault.

In Washington, D.C. at 1:47 P.M. local time, Secretary of the Navy Frank Knox telephoned FDR to announce, "Mr. President, it looks as if the Japanese have attacked Pearl Harbor."

Lines hummed, wheels turned, and frenzy mounted. When FDR told Aide Harry Hopkins about the report, Hopkins couldn't believe it. "It was just the kind of unexpected thing the Japanese would do," the President said. "At the very time they were discussing peace in the Pacific they were plotting to overthrow it."[6]

FDR immediately prepared to ask Congress to declare war on Japan, Germany, and Italy. Accordingly, on Monday, December 8, 1941, he addressed the nation. *"Yesterday, December 7, 1941, a date which will live in infamy, the United States was suddenly and deliberately attacked by naval and air forces of the Empire of Japan."*

The Japanese had hoped their Pearl Harbor assault would be a crippling blow that would remove any chance for the U.S. to recover. They were wrong, for despite the tremendous damage inflicted, not a single U.S. aircraft carrier was sunk. True, all eight battleships had been knocked out, along with three cruisers, and many destroyers; the U. S. no longer had a Pacific Fleet. A devastating blow, but the "date of infamy" became a rallying cry which galvanized Americans everywhere into action—to unite and ultimately to defeat the assailants and their cohorts.

END NOTES

Book I: State of the Nation
Chapter 1 (Prior Years)
[iii] For further details, see Ron Chernow, Titan: Life of John D. Rockefeller, Sr. NewYork: Vintage Books, 1999.
[2] New York Public Library Desk Reference, 2nd ed. New York: Prentice Hall General Reference, 1993, p. 771.
[3] World Almanac and Book of Facts for 1940. E. Eastman Irvine (ed.). New York: New York World-Telegram, 1940, p. 623.

Chapter 2 (Hard Times)
[1] Harvey Wish, Contemporary America, rev. ed. New York: Harper & Brothers, 1995, p. 491.
[2] These farm income figures are drawn from Statistical Abstract of the United States, 1935. Washington, D.C.: Government Printing Office.
[3] World Almanac and Book of Facts for 1940. E. Eastman Irvine (ed.). New York: New York World-Telegram, 1940, p. 640.
[4] Des Moines Sunday Register, October 27, 1996, p. 2A.
[5] Louis M. Hacker and Benjamin B. Kendrick. The United States Since 1865. New York: F. S. Crofts & Co., 1935, pp. 728-29.

Chapter 3 (Daily Lives)
[1] Timothy Egan. The Worst Hard Time. Boston: Houghton Mifflin Co., 2006, p. 35.
[2] Loc. cit., p. 77.
[3] Wish, op. cit., p. 491.
[4] For example, see Little Heathens, especially Chapter 4. New York: Bantam Dell, 2008, pp. 40-48.
[5] William Manchester. American Caesar: Douglas MacArthur 1880-1964. New York: Dell Publishing Co., 1978, pp. 164-65.
[6] *Ibid.*

Chapter 4 (A Mobile Society)
[1] As quoted in The Big Change. New York: Harper & Brothers, 1952, p. 117.
[2] *Ibid.*, p.121
[3] World Almanac and Book of Facts for 2005. William A. McGiveran, Jr. (ed.). New York: World Almanac Education Group, Inc., 2005, p. 237.
[4] World Almanac for 1940, E. Eastman Irvine (ed.). New York: New York World-Telegram, 1940, p. 555.
[5] There are no precise figures for average family income prior to 1935. Figures used herein are based on estimates prepared by the National Resources Committee in 1940.
[6] As quoted in Studs Terkel, My American Century. New York: The New Press, 1997, p. 121.

Chapter 5 (Fringe Elements)

[1] Hal Elliott Wert. Hoover: The Fishing President. Mechanicsburg, Pennsylvania: Stackpole Books, 2005, p. 93.

[2] Facts About the Presidents, Joseph Nathan Kane, ed. New York: Permabooks, 1959, p. 331.

[3] Quoted by Wish, *op. cit.*, p. 414.

[4] Kenneth S. Davis. FDR: The New Deal Years 1933-1937. New York: Random House, 1979, p. 495.

[5] Arthur M. Schlesinger, Jr. The Politics of Upheaval. Boston: Houghton Mifflin Co., 1960, p. 65.

[6] Davis, *op. cit.*, p. 575.

Chapter 6 (Expanding Horizons)

[1] Cabell Phillips. From the Crash to the Blitz 1929-1939. New York: The Macmillan Company, 1969, p. 339.

[2] *Ibid.*, pp. 171-72.

[3] Bryan B. Sterling and Frances N. Sterling. Will Rogers and Wiley Post: Death at Barrow. Manhattan, New York: M. Evans & Company, 1993.

Chapter 7 (Entertainment & Recreation)

[1] Elizabeth McLeod. The Original Amos n' Andy: Freeman Gosden, Charles Correll and the 1928-1943 Radio Serial. Jefferson, North Carolina: The McFarland & Co., 2005.

[2] Paul White. News on the Air. New York: Harcourt, Brace, and Co., 1947, pp. 301-02.

[3] As quoted in Triumph, a book about the 1936 Olympics, written by Jeremy Schaap.

[4] The sketch of Joe Louis's career is drawn largely from two books: Chris Mead, Champion—Joe Louis, Black Hero in White America, New York: Scribner, 1985, and Joe Louis Barrow, Jr., Joe Louis: Fifty Years an   American Hero, New York: McGraw-Hill, 1988.

[5] Peter Conn. Pearl S. Buck: A Cultural Biography. Cambridge, MA: Cambridge University, 1966.

[6] World Almanac for 2005, p. 328.

[7] Holly Knox. Sally Rand: From Film to Fans. New York: Maverick Press, 1988.

[8] Robert Dallek. Lone Star Rising: Lyndon Johnson and His Times 1908-1960. New York: Oxford University Press, 1991, p. 77.

[9] Quoted by Robert Underhill. The Bully Pulpit. New York: Vantage Press, 1988, p. 389.

Chapter 8. (Crime & Criminals)

[1] Samuel Eliot Morison. The Oxford History of the American People. New York: Oxford University Press, 1965, p. 901.

[2] Wayne Curtis. And a Bottle of Rum. New York: Crown Publishing Group, 2006, pp. 156-57.

[3] World Almanac for 1940, p. 639.

[4] *Ibid.*, p. 640.

[5] Ron Tyler, (ed.). The New Handbook of Texas, vol. 1. Austin, Texas: Texas State Historical Association, 1996, p. 396.

[6] Curt Gentry. J. Edgar Hoover: The Man and the Secrets. New York: W. W. Norton & Company, 1991, pp. 170-71.

[7] "Dillinger Slain in Chicago: Shot Dead by Federal Men in Front of Movie Theatre," New York Times, July 22, 1934.

[8] John Wasik. The Merchant of Power: Samuel Insull, Thomas Edison, and the Creation of the Modern Metropolis. New York: Palgrave McMillan Publishers, 2006.

Chapter 9 (Racial Stirrings)

[1] Harvey Wish. Contemporary America, rev. ed. New York: Harper and Brothers, 1955, p. 499.

[2] Gunnar Myrdal. An American Dilemma: The Negro Problem and Modern Democracy.

[3] See, Douglas O.Linder. "Without Fear or Favor: Judge James Horton and the Scottsboro Boys." Essays found under *D. Linder, The Scottsboro Boys Trials. Internet:umkc.edu*

[4] Journal Gazette, Ft. Wayne, Indiana, March 15, 1998, Section C.

[5] *Ibid.*

Chapter 10 (Labor Unions)

[1] Ray Ginger, The Bending Cross. Chicago, Illinois: Haymarket Books, 2007, pp. 398-405.

[2] Manchester, Glory and the Dream, p. 160.

[3] As quoted by William Safire, Lend Me Your Ears: Great Speeches in History. New York: W. W. Norton & Co., 1992, pp. 584-86.

[4] Morison, *op. cit.*, p. 979.

Chapter 11 (Entry of Franklin Roosevelt)

[1] Sara Roosevelt. My Boy Franklin. New York: Ray Long and Richard Smith, 1933, p. 12.

[2] Geoffrey C. Ward. A First Class Temperament: The Emergence of Franklin Roosevelt. New York: Book-of-the-Month Club by arrangement with the author, 1989, p. 131.

[3] World Almanac for 1940, p. 639.

Chapter 12 (The Big Change)

[1] The Public Papers and Public Addresses of Franklin D. Roosevelt, ed. Samuel I. Rosenman. New York: Random House, 1938, vol. p. 647.

[2] Samuel Rosenman. Working With Roosevelt. New York: Da Capo Press, 1972, p. 71.

[3] Encyclopedia of American History, Richard B. Morris, ed. New York: Harper &

Bros., 1953,   p. 341.

[4] Kenneth S. Davis. FDR: The New Deal Years 1933-1937. New York: Random House, 1979, p. 25.

[5] Robert Underhill. The Bully Pulpit. New York: Vantage Press, 1988., p. 18.

Chapter 13 (Early New Deal)

[1] Frank Freidel, America in the Twentieth Century. New York: Alfred A. Knopf, 1976, p. 177.

[2] Morison, *op. cit.*, p. 979.

[3] Statistical Abstract of the United States 1934. p. 37.

[4] Cf. Milton Friedman and Anna Jacobson Schwartz, A Monetary History of the United States, 1867-1960. Princeton, New Jersey: Princeton University Press, 1963, pp. 434-37, *passim.*

[5] Encyclopedia of American History, p. 342.

[6] *Ibid.*

[7] Robert E. Sherwood. Roosevelt and Hopkins: An Intimate History. New York: Harper & Brothers, 1948, p. 33.

[8] *Time,* November 13, 2008.

[9] Davis, *op. cit.,* pp. 120-21.

[10] Wish, *op. cit.,* p. 447.

Chapter 14 (FDR's Second Administration)

[1] As quoted by Joseph P. Lash, Eleanor & Franklin. New York: W. W. Norton & Co., 1971, p. 522.

[2] Quoted by Ted Morgan in FDR—A Biography. New York: Simon & Schuster, 1985, p. 385.

[3] David E.Lilienthal, TVA: Democracy on the March. New York: Harper & Bros., 1944.

Chapter 15 (Security for the Aged)

[1] Frances Perkins. The Roosevelt I Knew. New York: Penguin Group, 1946.

[2] World Almanac and Book of Facts for 1940. E. Eastman Irvine, (ed.). New York: New York World-Telegram, 1940, p. 741.

[3] *Steward Machine Company v. Davis*, 301 U.S. 548 (1937). Retrieved on December 3, 2005.

[4] *Ibid.*

[5] Helvering v. Davis, 301 U.S. 619 (1937). Retrieved on December 3, 2005.

Chapter 16 (Supreme Court Imbroglio)

[1] Encyclopedia of American History, Richard B. Morris, ed. New York: Harper & Brothers, 1953, p. 345.

[2] Nathan Miller, FDR: An Intimate History. New York: Doubleday & Company, Inc., 1983. Pp. 370-73, *passim.*

[3] The speech was delivered by W. J. Cameron, speaking over CBS on the Ford Hour, 1936.

[4] H. L. Mencken, "Three Years of Dr. Roosevelt," American Mercury, March 1936.
[5] Schlesinger, p. 580.
[6] Facts About the Presidents, p. 343.
[7] Rosenman, op. cit., pp. 158-59.
[8] Robert Dallek. Lone Star Rising: Lyndon Johnson and His Times 1908-1960. New York: Oxford University Press, 1991, p. 179-80.

Book II: Storms Approaching
Chapter 17 (Warning Clouds)
[1] Father Edmund A. Walsh, Rector of Georgetown University to Air Force Officers at the Institute of Linguistics, Washington, D.C., February, 1952.
[2] Allen, Only Yesterday, pp. 38-39.
[3] Alexander Leitch. A Princeton Companion. Princeton, New Jersey: Princeton University Press, 1978.
[4] Quoted as ". . . evidence of the decadence and corrupt condition of democracy." Richard J. Hand, Terror on the Air: Horror Radio in America—1931-1952. Jefferson, North Carolina: McFarlane and Co., 2006, p.7.
[5] Albert Einstein's letter to President Roosevelt, dated August 2, 1939, is located in the "America Since Hoover" Collection at the Franklin D. Roosevelt Library, Hyde Park, N.Y.
[6] Accounts of this historic meeting when Alexander Sachs transmitted Einstein's letter to FDR can be found in numerous histories or biographies. My account is taken largely from Richard Rhodes, The Making of the Atomic Bomb, pp. 291-315, *passim.*

Chapter 18 (Aid to Britain)
[1] World Almanac for 2005, p. 521.
[2] Nathan Miller. FDR: An Intimate History. New York: Doubleday & Co., Inc., 1983, pp. 403-04.
[3] Washington Post, December 30, 1940.
[4] Public Papers and Addresses of Franklin D. Roosevelt. Vol. 9., pp. 607-08.
[5] Ted Morgan. FDR: A Biography. New York: Simon & Schuster, 1985, pp. 597-98.
[6] Richard B. Morris. Encyclopedia of American History. New York: Harper & Bros., 1953, p. 367.
[7] As quoted by Ted Morgan, op. cit., p. 601.

Chapter 19 (Campaign of 1940)
[1] As quoted by Davis, FDR: Into the Storm 1937-1940. New York: Random House, 1993, p. 437.
[2] *Ibid.*, pp. 437-38.
[3] Richard Ketchum. The Borrowed Years 1938-1941. New York: Random House, 1989, p. 180.
[4] Sherwood, Roosevelt and Hopkins, p. 226.
[5] Public Papers of Franklin D. Roosevelt, vol. 8., p. 455.

[6] Davis, *op. cit.*, pp. 456-57.

[7] William Manchester wrote, "Above all, he [Willkie] should never have been subjected to the accusation from Henry Wallace, FDR's new vice-presidential candidate, that Willkie was the Nazis' choice." The Glory and the Dream, p. 226.

[8] *Ibid.*, p. 225.

[9] Morgan, *op. cit.*, pp. 533-34.

Chapter 20 (Eve of Infamy)

[1] Harry S Truman. Memoirs by Harry S Truman. Vol. 1. New York: Doubleday & Company, Inc., 1955, pp. 227-28. In these Memoirs President reported that on May 8, 1945, the day war in Europe officially ended, Leo Crowley, Foreign Economic Advisor, and Acting Secretary of State Joseph C. Grew came into the Oval Office and informed him that the original Lend Lease Act authorized the President to cut back on the volume of Lend Lease supplies when Germany surrendered. Truman wrote further: "What they told me made good sense to me; with Germany out of the war, Lend Lease should be reduced. . . I reached for my pen and, without reading the document, I signed it."

[2] Joseph C. Grew, Turbulent Era: A Diplomatic Record of Forty Years, 1904-1945. Boston: Houghton Mifflin, 1952, p. 1233.

[3] U. S. Department of Defense, "The 'Magic' Background of Pearl Harbor," p. 66. National Archives.

[4] Morison, *op. cit.*, p. 1000.

[5] Gordon W. Prange. At Dawn We Slept. New York: McGraw, 1981, pp. 371-72.

[6] As quoted by Nathan Miller, *op. cit.*, p. 477. Also cf. Roosevelt and Hopkins, pp. 426-27.

BIBLIOGRAPHY

Allen, Frederick Lewis. Only Yesterday. New York: Harper & Row, 1931.

Allen, Frederick Lewis. The Big Change. New York: Harper & Brothers, 1952.

_____. Only Yesterday. New York: Harper & Row, 1931.

Beard, Charles A. American Foreign Policy in the Making, 1932-1940. New Haven: Yale University Press, 1946.

Chang, Iris. The Rape of Nanking. New York: Penguin Books, 1997.

Chernow, Ron. Titan: The Life of John D. Rockefeller, Sr. New York: Vintage Books, 1999.

Conn, Peter. Pearl S. Buck: A Cultural Biography. Cambridge, Ma.: Cambridge University Press, 1966.

Cooke, Alistair. The American Home Front 1941-1942. New York: Grove Press, 2006.

Curtis, Wayne. And a Bottle of Rum. New York: Crown Publishing Group, 2006.

Dallek, Robert. Lone Star Rising: Lyndon Johnson and His Times 1908-1960. New York: Oxford University Press, 1991.

Defenders of Liberty: 2nd Bombardment Group/Wing 1918-1993. Paducah, Kentucky: Turner Publishing Company, 1996.

Dubofsky, Melvin and Warren Van Tine. John L. Lewis: A Biography. Champaign,

Illinois: University of Illinois Press, 1986.)

Egan, Timothy. The Worst Hard Time. New York: Mariner Books, 2006.

Encyclopedia of World History. William L. Langer, ed. New York: Houghton Mifflin Co., 1948.

Freidel, Frank. America in the Twentieth Century. New York: Alfred A. Knopf, 1976.

Gentry, Curt. J. Edgar Hoover: The Man and the Secrets. New York: W. W. Norton & Company, 1991.

Ginger, Ray. The Bending Cross. Chicago, Illinois, 2007, pp. 398-405.

Hamilton, Carl. In No Time At All. Ames, Iowa: Iowa State University Press, 1974.

Hochmuth, Marie Kathryn, (ed.). A History and Criticism opf American Public Address, vol. III. New York: Longmans, Green and Co., 1955.

Kalish, Mildred Armstrong. Little Heathens. New York: Bantam Books, 2008.

Ketchum, Richard M. The Borrowed Years 1938-1941. New York: Random House, 1989.

Korda, Michael. Making the List: A Cultural History of the American Bestseller 1900-1999.

New York: Barnes & Noble Publishing, Inc., 2001.

Larson, Erik. The Devil in the White City. New York: Vintage Books, 2004.

Lash, Joseph P. Eleanor and Franklin. NewYork: W. W. Norton & Co., 1971.

Leitch, Alexander. A Princeton Companion. Princeton, New Jersey: Princeton University Press, 1978.

Lilienthal, David E. TVA: Democracy on the March. New York: Harper & Bros., 1944.

Linder, Douglas O. "Without Fear or Favor: Judge James Horton and the Scottsboro Boys." Essays found under D. Linder, The Scottsboro Boys Trials. Internet:umkc.edu

Manchester, William. American Caesar: Douglas MacArthur 1880-1964. New York: Dell Publishing, 1978.

_____. The Glory and The Dream. Vol. II. Boston: Little, Brown, and Company, 1973.

McLeod, Elizabeth. The Original Amos n' Andy: Freeman Gosden, Charles Correll, and the 928-1943 Radio Serial. Jefferson, North Carolina: McFarland & Co., 2005.

Miller, Nathan. FDR: An Intimate History. New York: Doubleday & Company, 1983.

Morgan, Ted. FDR: A Biography. New York: Simon & Schuster, 1985.

Morison, Samuel Eliot. The Oxford History of the American People. New York: Oxford University Press, 1965.

Morris, Richard B. (ed.). Encyclopedia of American History. New York: Harper & Brothers, 1953.

New York Public Library Desk Reference. 2nd ed. New York: Prentice Hall General Reference, 1933.

Nothing to Fear, ed. B. C. Zevin. Boston: Houghton Mifflin, 1946.

Neal, Steve. Dark Horse: A Biography of Wendell Willkie. Garden City, New York: Doubleday, 1984.

Parmet, Herbert S. and Marie B. Hecht. Never Again: A President Runs for a Third

Term. New York: Macmillan & Co., 1968.

Perkins, Frances. The Roosevelt I Knew. New York: Penguin Group, 1946.

Phillips, Cabell. From the Crash to the Blitz 1929-1939. New York: The Macmillan Company, 1969.

Prange, Gordon W. At Dawn We Slept. New York: McGraw, 1981.

Reagan Ronald and Richard G. Hubler. Where's the Rest of Me? New York: Duell, Sloan, and Pearce, 1985.

Rhodes, Richard. The Making of the Atomic Bomb. New York: Simon & Schuster, 1986.

Roosevelt, Sara. My Boy Franklin. New York: Ray Long and Richard Smith, 1933.

Rosenman, Samuel I. Working With Roosevelt. New York: Da Capo Press, 1972.

Rosenman, Samuel I. (ed.). 13 vols. The Public Papers and Addresses of Franklin D. Roosevelt. New York: Random House, 1938.

Safire, William. Lend Me Your Ears: Great Speeches in History. New York: W. W. Norton & Co., 1992.

Schaap, Jeremy. Triumph: the 1936 Olympics. Boston: Houghton Miffline, 2007.

Statistical Abstract of the United States 1934. Washington, D.C.: United States Census Bureau, 1935.

Schlesinger, Arthur M. Jr. The Politics of Upheaval: The Age of Roosevelt. Boston: Houghton Mifflin Company, 1960.

Sherwood, Robert E. Roosevelt and Hopkins, An Intimate History. New York: Harper & Brothers, 1948.

Sterling, Bryan B. and Frances N. Sterling. Will Rogers and Wiley Post: Death at Barrow. Manhattan, New York: M. Evans & Company, 1993.

Stone, Irving. Adversary in the House. Garden City, New York: Doubleday & Co., Inc., 1947.

Terkel, Studs. My American Century. New York: The New Press, 1997.

Toland, John. Adolph Hitler. New York: Ballantine Books, 1977.

Truman, Harry S. Memoirs of Harry S Truman: Year of Decisions. New York: Doubleday & Co., 1955.

_____. Memoirs of Harry S Truman: Years of Trial and Hope. New York: Doubleday & Co., 1956.

Tyler, Ron. (ed.). The New Handbook of Texas. Vol. 1. Austin: Texas: Texas State Historical Association, 1996.

Underhill, Robert. FDR and Harry: Parallel Lives. Westport, CT: Praeger Publishers, 1996.

_____. Meanwhile at Home—1941-1945. Ames, Iowa: Sigler Company, 2007.

_____. The Bully Pulpit. New York: Vantage Press, 1988.

Ward, Geoffrey C. A First Class Temperament: The Emergence of Franklin Roosevelt. New York: Book-of-the-Month Club, 1989.

Wasik, John. The Merchant of Power: Samuel Insull, Thomas A. Edison, and the Creation of the Modern Metropolis. New York: Palgrave McMillan Publishers, 2006.

Wert, Hal Elliott. Hoover: The Fishing President. Mechanicsburg, Pennsylvania: Stackpole Books, 2005.

White, Paul W. News on the Air. New York: Harcourt, Brace, and Company, 1947.

White, William Allen. A Puritan in Babylon. New York: The MacMillan Company, 1958.

Williams, T. Harry. Huey Long. New York: Vintage Books, 2006.

Wish, Harvey. Contemporary America: The National Scene Since 1900. New York: Harper & Brothers, 1948.

_____. Contemporary America: The National Scene Since 1900. Rev. ed. New York: Harper & Brothers, 1955.

World Almanac and Book of Facts for 1940. E. Eastman Irvine (ed.). New York: New York World-Telegram, 1940.

World Almanac and Book of Facts for 2005. William A. McGiveren, Jr. (ed.). New York:World Almanac Education Group, Inc., 2005.

Zevin, B. D. (ed.). Nothing To Fear: Selected Addresses of Franklin Delano Roosevelt. New York: Houghton Mifflin Co., 1946.

Newspapers & Magazines

Des Moines Register

Ft. Wayne, Indiana, Journal Gazette

Life

Newsweek

New York Times

Saturday Evening Post

Time

Wallace's Farmer

Washington Post

INDEX

radio, 29-30,
    Amos n' Andy, 29-30
    "Kingfish" George Stevens, 29
    Marx brothers, 31
  sports, 32-36
    press vs. radio, 32-33
"every man a king," 24

Gompers, Samuel, 56
"Gone With the Wind," 31
Gosden, Freeman F., 29
Graf Zeppelin, 28
Great Depression, xi, 18
    Price drops during the depression, 7-8
Greeley, Horace, 14
Grew, Joseph C., 112

H

Hamer, Frank, 46
Hamilton, Polly, 47
Hamilton, Raymond, 45
Hamm, William, 45
Harding, Warren G., 3, 18, 19-20
Hart, Brook I., 45
Hauptmann, Bruno Richard, 44
Hawks, Frank, 27
Heater, Gabriel, 29
Heline, Oscar, 17
Herman, Woody, 32
Hindenburg disaster, 28
Hitler, Adolph, xii, 34, 92, 94-95, 96 , 97-99
    (Hitler Cont.), 105
Hoffman, Harold G., 44
Holmes, John, 45
Home Owner's Loan Act, 71
Home Owner's Refinancing Act (HOLC) 78-79
Homestead Acts, 9
Hoover, Herbert C., 4,5-8, 12,16, 18-21, 43
    (Hoover, cont.), 63, 66, 67, 69, 86, 89
Hoover, J. Edgar, 47
Hoover, Lou, 19
Hopkins, Harry, 72-73, 101, 115
Horton, James, 52-53
Howard, Leslie, 31
Howard, Roy, 107
Howe, Louis, 63
Hughes, Charles Evans, 90
Hull, Cordell, 74
"Hundred Days," 69, 71
Husing, Ted, 33

I

Ickes, Harold, 82, 84-85

Immigrants, 1,2
   Irish immigrants 1
Insull, Samuel, 48
Iowa milk strike, 6-7
"Iowa will go Methodist," 17
"I Won't Work," 93

J

Jackson, Robert, 89
James, Harry, 32
Japan-Germany-Italy Pact, 111
Japan invasion of China, 112
Jefferson, Thomas, 88
Jessel, George, 38
Johnson, Charles S. 50
Johnson, Hiram, 22, 86, 105
Johnson, Hugh, 84-85
Johnson, Jack, 34
Johnson, Lyndon B., 40, 91
Jones, William Daniel, 46

K

Kaltenborn, H. V., 29
Karpis-Barker Gang, 45
Kellogg-Briand Pact, 92
Kelly, Edward, 59
Kelly, George "Machine Gun," 44
Kennedy, John F., 40
Keynes, John Maynard, xii, 73-74, 106
Kidnappings, 43-45
Kimmel, Husband, 114
King Kong, 4
Knight, Thomas, 52
Knights of Labor, 56
Knox, Frank, 86, 115
Knudsen, William S., 111
Konoye, Fumimaro, 113
Krock, Arthur, 73-74
Kuhn, Fritz Julius, 98
Ku Klux Klan, 2, 50, 54-55
Kurusu, Saburo, 113

L

Labor Strikes, 57-60

General Motors strike, 59
steel company strikes, 58-59
LaFollette, Robert M., 59
LaGuardia, Fiorello, 32
Landon, Alfred, 86-97
Lazarus, Emma, 1
Lehmann, Emil, 28
Leigh, Vivian, 31
LeMay, Curtis, 97
Lend Lease,73, 106, 111
Lewis, John L., 57-58, 59-60
Lewis, Sinclair, 36
Liebowitz, Samuel, 52
Lilienthal, David, 77
Limericks, 6
Lincoln, Abraham, xi, 88
Lindbergh, Anne Morrow, 43
Lindbergh, Charles A., 26-27, 43-44, 97
Lippmann, Walter, 64
Lombard, Carole, 31
Lombardo, Guy 32
Long, Huey, 22-24, 48, 81
Lossing, John, 37
Louis, Joe, 34-36
Luce, Henry, 36
Luciano, Salvatore "Lucky," 41-42
Luer, August, 44

M

MacAdoo, William, 63
MacArthur, Douglas, 12, 113
Maginot Line, 99
Maguires, Molly, 56
Manhattan Project, 95-96
Marion, Indiana, 54
Marriage & Divorce rates, 10
Marshall, George, 102
Martin, Joseph, 108
Marx, Karl, 24, 73
Mattern, James, 27
McElroy, Mary, 44
McGee, Walter, 44
McKinley Tariff, 16
McNary, Charles L., 107
Melchior, Lauritz, 32

Mencken, H. L., 22, 43, 86
Miller, Glenn, 32
Minnesota mortgages, 6
Mitchell, Margaret, 31
Mitchell, William "Billy), 97
Moley, Raymond, 66
Monnet, Jean, 106
Moran, George "Bugs," 42-43
Morgan, J. P., 79
Morgenthau, Henry, 74
Murray, "Alfalfa" Bill, 63
Muscle Shoals, 77-78
Mussolini, Benito, 92, 94-95, 105, 108
Myrdal, Gunnar, 50

Planck, Max, 95-96
Pocketbooks, 36
Poland Invaded & subdued, 99
"Poor Laws," 80-81
Population growth, 5,10,
   growth in Panhandle, 9
   shifts, 14
Post, Wiley, 2
Powell, Ozzie, 52
Prelude, xi, xii
Presidential election 1928, 20
Presidential election, 1936, 87
Price fallings, 7
Price, Victoria, 51-52
Prohibition, 41-43
Pruss, Max, 28
Public Works Administration (PWA), 84
Purvis, Melvin, 47

   R
Radcliff College, 93-94
Rand, Sally, 38
Rayburn, Samuel, 88, 91
Reconstruction Finance Corp. (RFC), 21, 69
Red Scare, 3
Regan, Ronald, 35-36, 40
Reid, Ogden, 107
Remarque, Erich Maria, 30
Rethberg, Elisabeth, 32
Ribbentrop, Joachim von, 39
Richthofen, Manfred, 97
Rickenbacker, Eddie, 97
Robinson, Joe, 20, 23, 88
Robinson, Thomas H., 45
Rock, Joe, 42
Rockefeller, John D., 1
Rogers, Will, 27, 67
Rommel, Erwin, 100
Roosevelt, Alice Longworth, 3
Roosevelt, Claes Martenszen, 61,
Roosevelt, Eleanor, 64
Roosevelt, Franklin D., 4-5, 19, 21-22, 43, 57, 58-60
   (Roosevelt, cont.), 61-62, 64, 65-68, 76, 85
   (cont.) 95, 99-100, 108, 112-113, 115

Roosevelt, James, 61-62
Roosevelt, Sara Delano, 62, 102
Roosevelt, Theodore, 19, 62, 64
Rosenman, Samuel, 65, 88
Rural Electrification Act, 90-91
Ruth, Babe, 98

S

Sachs, Alexander, 96
Sage, Anna, 47
Saturday Evening Post, 15
Schecter Poultry Corporation, 85
Schmeling, Max, 34-35
Schorr, Friedrich, 32
Schultz, Arthur "Dutch," 42
Scottsboro Boys, 51-53
Selective Service Act, 102
"Share the Wealth," 23
Sharkey, Jack, 35
Shaw, George Bernard, 30
Sherwood, Robert, 30
Shipp, Thomas, 54
Short, Walter, 114
Simpson, Wallis Warfield, 39
Sitzkrieg (Phony War), 99
Smith, Abram, 54
Smith, Adam, xii, 73
Smith, Alfred E., 4, 20, 63, 72, 81
Smith, Gerald L. K., 22
Smoot-Hawley Tariff, 16
Social Security Act, 82-83
Socialist Party in America, 93-94
Society, 3
Soviets attack Finland, 99
Stalin, Josef, 93, 100
Stassen, Harold, 107
Steagall, Henry, 79
Steinbeck, John, 38
Stephenson, David, 54-55
St. Louis Post-Dispatch, 59
Sterling, Bryan & Frances, 27
Steward Machine Company, 82
Stimson, Henry, 114
Stock Market, 4
    Exchanges during crash, 8

U.S.S. Condor, 115
U.S.S. Greer, 102
U.S.S. Kearney, 102-103
U.S. Supreme Court, 82-83, 85-90

V

Valentine Day Massacre, 42-43
Vallee, Rudy, 3
Vandenberg, Arthur H., 86, 106
Vanderbilts, 61
Van Doren, Irita, 109
Vietnam War, 94

W

Wabash, Indiaana, 3
Wall Street, 3-4,
Wallace, Henry, 74, 109
Walsh, Edmund, 93
Walsh, Richard, 37-38
Warnings about Japan, 112 -113, 115
Washington, Booker T., 51
Washington, George, 104
Weddell, J. R., 27
Wehrmacht, 95
Weiss, Carl Austin, 24
Welles, Orson, 94
Wheat crops, 9-10
Wheeler Air Field, 115
Wheeler, Burton, 89-90
White, Paul, 33
Whiteman, Paul, 32
White Slave Traffic Act, 47
Whitney, Courtney, 12-13
Wigner, Eugene, 96
Wilkie, Wendell, 105-106, 107-110
Wilkins, Roy, 51
Wilson, Woodrow, 41, 62, 64, 87, 92
Woodin, William H., 66
Woolworth Store, 15
Women voting, 3
"Women's work," 11-12
Wright, Roy, 51

Y

Yamamoto, Admiral, 114-115

Young, Owen D., 63